50 French Pastry Simplified Recipes for Home

By: Kelly Johnson

Table of Contents

- Croissants
- Pain au Chocolat
- Éclairs
- Macarons
- Tarte Tatin
- Madeleines
- Profiteroles
- Palmiers
- Mille-feuille
- Choux à la Crème (Cream Puffs)
- Financiers
- Pâte à Choux
- Cannele
- Brioche
- Pain de Campagne (French Country Bread)
- Quiche Lorraine
- Galettes des Rois (King Cake)
- Clafoutis
- Soufflé
- Tarte au Citron (Lemon Tart)
- Chouquettes
- Paris-Brest
- Gougères
- Bûche de Noël (Yule Log)
- Kouign-Amann
- Pithiviers
- Tarte aux Fraises (Strawberry Tart)
- Palmiers
- Canelés de Bordeaux
- Pain Perdu (French Toast)
- Tarte Normande
- Tarte aux Pommes (Apple Tart)
- Crème Brûlée
- Mousse au Chocolat
- Pralines
- Galette Bretonne

- Tarte à la Rhubarbe (Rhubarb Tart)
- Beignets
- Flan Parisien
- Pain d'Épices (French Spice Bread)
- Saint-Honoré
- Navettes de Marseille
- Tuiles
- Petits Fours
- Opéra Cake
- Cherry Clafoutis
- Croquembouche
- Brioche aux Pralines
- Tarte Tropézienne
- Pâte Feuilletée (Puff Pastry)

Croissants

Ingredients:

- 2 1/4 cups (280g) all-purpose flour, plus extra for dusting
- 1/4 cup (50g) granulated sugar
- 1 tsp salt
- 1 tbsp active dry yeast
- 3/4 cup (180ml) warm water
- 1/2 cup (120g) vegan butter or margarine, cold and cut into cubes
- 1/2 cup (120g) vegan butter or margarine, softened (for rolling)
- 1 tbsp non-dairy milk, for brushing

Instructions:

1. **Activate the Yeast:**
   - In a small bowl, combine the warm water, sugar, and yeast. Let it sit for about 5-10 minutes until frothy.
2. **Prepare the Dough:**
   - In a large mixing bowl, whisk together the flour and salt. Add the frothy yeast mixture and stir until a dough forms.
3. **Incorporate Cold Butter:**
   - Transfer the dough to a lightly floured surface and knead for about 5 minutes until smooth and elastic. Shape the dough into a ball, cover with plastic wrap, and refrigerate for 30 minutes.
4. **Make the Butter Block:**
   - While the dough is chilling, place the cold cubed vegan butter between two sheets of parchment paper. Using a rolling pin, pound and roll the butter into a 6x6-inch square. Place the butter block in the refrigerator to chill.
5. **Roll and Fold the Dough:**
   - On a lightly floured surface, roll out the chilled dough into a 10x10-inch square. Place the chilled butter block diagonally on the dough square, so it looks like a diamond. Fold the corners of the dough over the butter to enclose it completely.
6. **Create Layers (First Turn):**
   - Roll out the dough into a rectangle about 12x18 inches. Fold the dough into thirds like a letter (bottom third up, then top third down). This completes the first turn.
7. **Chill and Repeat:**
   - Wrap the dough in plastic wrap and refrigerate for 30 minutes. Repeat the rolling and folding process (second turn).
8. **Shape the Croissants:**
   - Roll out the dough to 1/4-inch thickness. Cut triangles with a base of about 4 inches and height of about 8 inches. Make a small cut in the base of each triangle and gently stretch it.
9. **Roll and Proof:**

- Starting at the base, roll each triangle up towards the point to form a croissant shape. Place the shaped croissants on a baking sheet lined with parchment paper, leaving space between them. Cover with a clean kitchen towel and let them rise in a warm place for about 1-2 hours until doubled in size.

10. **Bake the Croissants:**
    - Preheat your oven to 400°F (200°C).
    - Brush the tops of the croissants with non-dairy milk.
    - Bake for 15-18 minutes, or until golden brown and flaky.
11. **Cool and Enjoy:**
    - Let the croissants cool on a wire rack for a few minutes before serving warm. Enjoy your homemade vegan croissants!

These croissants may not be as intricate as traditional versions, but they still deliver a delicious buttery flavor and flaky texture, making them perfect for a cozy breakfast or brunch treat.

Pain au Chocolat

Ingredients:

- 1 sheet of puff pastry (store-bought or homemade)
- 12 small sticks of dark chocolate (or chocolate chips)
- 1 egg, beaten (for egg wash)
- Optional: powdered sugar for dusting

Instructions:

1. **Prepare the Puff Pastry:**
    - If using store-bought puff pastry, thaw it according to the package instructions. If making homemade puff pastry, follow your recipe to prepare and roll out the pastry dough into a rectangle about 1/8 inch thick.
2. **Cut and Shape the Dough:**
    - Using a sharp knife or a pizza cutter, cut the pastry into rectangles, about 3 inches wide and 5-6 inches long.
3. **Add Chocolate:**
    - Place one or two pieces of chocolate at the edge of each rectangle (the shorter side). Roll the pastry tightly over the chocolate, folding the sides in as you go, until the chocolate is completely enclosed.
4. **Arrange on Baking Sheet:**
    - Place each Pain au Chocolat seam-side down on a baking sheet lined with parchment paper, leaving space between them to expand.
5. **Egg Wash:**
    - Brush the tops of the pastries lightly with beaten egg using a pastry brush. This will give them a golden-brown color when baked.
6. **Bake:**
    - Preheat your oven to 400°F (200°C). Bake the Pain au Chocolat for 15-18 minutes, or until they are puffed up and golden brown.
7. **Cool and Serve:**
    - Remove from the oven and let cool on a wire rack. Optionally, dust with powdered sugar before serving.

Notes:

- **Puff Pastry:** Using good quality puff pastry is key to achieving flaky and delicious Pain au Chocolat. If making your own puff pastry, ensure it's well chilled and handle it gently to preserve the layers.
- **Chocolate:** Traditionally, dark chocolate sticks or batons are used for Pain au Chocolat. You can also use chocolate chips or chop a chocolate bar into small pieces.
- **Variations:** Some bakers like to sprinkle the Pain au Chocolat with coarse sugar before baking for added sweetness and crunch.

Enjoy your homemade Pain au Chocolat!

Éclairs

Ingredients:

For the Choux Pastry:

- 1/2 cup (1 stick) unsalted butter
- 1 cup water
- 1 cup all-purpose flour
- 4 large eggs

For the Pastry Cream:

- 2 cups whole milk
- 1/2 cup granulated sugar
- 4 large egg yolks
- 1/4 cup cornstarch
- 1 tsp vanilla extract

For the Chocolate Ganache:

- 1/2 cup heavy cream
- 4 oz dark chocolate, chopped
- 1 tbsp unsalted butter

Instructions:

Making the Choux Pastry:

1. **Preheat and Prepare:**
   - Preheat your oven to 400°F (200°C). Line a baking sheet with parchment paper.
2. **Make the Dough:**
   - In a medium saucepan, combine the butter and water over medium heat. Bring to a boil, then remove from heat and quickly stir in the flour until the mixture forms a ball and pulls away from the sides of the pan.
3. **Add Eggs:**
   - Transfer the dough to a mixing bowl. Beat in the eggs one at a time, mixing well after each addition, until the dough is smooth and glossy.
4. **Pipe and Bake:**
   - Transfer the dough to a piping bag fitted with a large round tip (or use a resealable plastic bag with a corner cut off). Pipe the dough into 4-5 inch long strips on the prepared baking sheet, leaving space between them.
5. **Bake:**

- Bake the éclairs in the preheated oven for 30-35 minutes, or until they are puffed up and golden brown. Remove from the oven and let cool completely on a wire rack.

Making the Pastry Cream:

1. **Heat Milk:**
   - In a medium saucepan, heat the milk over medium heat until it just begins to boil. Remove from heat.
2. **Mix Eggs and Sugar:**
   - In a mixing bowl, whisk together the sugar, egg yolks, and cornstarch until pale and thick.
3. **Temper and Cook:**
   - Gradually whisk the hot milk into the egg mixture. Pour the mixture back into the saucepan and cook over medium heat, stirring constantly, until it thickens and comes to a boil.
4. **Flavor:**
   - Remove from heat and stir in the vanilla extract. Transfer to a bowl and cover with plastic wrap directly on the surface to prevent a skin from forming. Chill in the refrigerator until cold.

Assembling the Éclairs:

1. **Fill the Éclairs:**
   - Once the éclairs have cooled completely, cut each one horizontally with a serrated knife. Spoon or pipe the chilled pastry cream into the bottom half of each éclair.
2. **Make the Ganache:**
   - In a small saucepan, heat the heavy cream until it just begins to boil. Remove from heat and add the chopped chocolate and butter. Let it sit for a minute, then stir until smooth and glossy.
3. **Glaze the Éclairs:**
   - Dip the top of each filled éclair into the chocolate ganache, letting any excess drip off. Place on a wire rack to allow the ganache to set.
4. **Serve:**
   - Serve the éclairs fresh. They can be refrigerated for a few hours, but are best enjoyed the same day they are made.

Notes:

- **Pastry Cream:** Make sure to chill the pastry cream thoroughly before filling the éclairs. This helps it set and makes filling easier.
- **Chocolate Ganache:** Adjust the thickness of the ganache by adding more cream for a thinner consistency or more chocolate for a thicker glaze.

- **Variations:** You can add different flavors to the pastry cream, such as coffee or almond extract, or decorate the éclairs with powdered sugar or additional toppings.

Enjoy your homemade Éclairs! They're a delightful treat perfect for any occasion.

Macarons

Ingredients:

For the Macaron Shells:

- 1 cup (100g) almond flour
- 1 3/4 cups (210g) powdered sugar
- 3 large egg whites, at room temperature
- 1/4 cup (50g) granulated sugar
- Gel food coloring (optional)

For the Filling:

- 1/2 cup (1 stick or 115g) unsalted butter, softened
- 1 cup (120g) powdered sugar
- 1-2 tbsp heavy cream (or milk)
- 1 tsp vanilla extract (or other flavoring of your choice)

Instructions:

Making the Macaron Shells:

1. **Prepare Baking Sheets:**
    - Line two baking sheets with parchment paper or silicone mats. You can also use macaron templates under the parchment paper to help guide the size of your macarons.
2. **Sift Dry Ingredients:**
    - In a medium bowl, sift together the almond flour and powdered sugar. This helps ensure a smooth macaron shell.
3. **Whip Egg Whites:**
    - In a clean, dry bowl of a stand mixer fitted with the whisk attachment, beat the egg whites on medium speed until foamy. Gradually add the granulated sugar, increase the speed to medium-high, and beat until stiff peaks form. The meringue should be glossy and hold its shape.
4. **Macaronage (Mixing):**
    - Add the sifted dry ingredients to the meringue. Using a rubber spatula, gently fold the dry ingredients into the meringue using a technique called macaronage. Fold and press the mixture against the sides of the bowl, rotating the bowl as you go, until the batter is smooth and shiny. Be careful not to overmix; the batter should flow like lava.
5. **Pipe the Macarons:**
    - Transfer the batter to a piping bag fitted with a round tip (usually about 1/2 inch in diameter). Pipe 1 to 1.5 inch rounds onto the prepared baking sheets, leaving space between each macaron.

6. **Resting the Macarons:**
   - Let the piped macarons rest at room temperature for about 30 minutes to 1 hour. This helps them develop a smooth top and form a skin, which is important for the feet (the ruffled edges) to form during baking.
7. **Bake:**
   - Preheat your oven to 300°F (150°C). Bake the macarons, one sheet at a time, for 15-18 minutes, rotating the baking sheet halfway through baking. The macarons are done when they are set and easily lift off the parchment paper. Let them cool completely on the baking sheet before removing.

Making the Filling:

1. **Prepare the Filling:**
   - In a mixing bowl, beat the softened butter until creamy. Gradually add the powdered sugar and beat until smooth and fluffy. Add the vanilla extract (or other flavoring) and heavy cream (or milk) as needed to achieve a smooth and spreadable consistency.
2. **Assemble the Macarons:**
   - Pair up the cooled macaron shells by size. Flip one shell of each pair over. Pipe or spoon a small amount of filling onto the center of the flipped shells. Gently press the remaining shells over the filling to create sandwiches.
3. **Mature the Macarons (Optional):**
   - Place the filled macarons in an airtight container in the refrigerator for 24-48 hours to "mature". This allows the flavors to meld and the texture to improve.
4. **Serve and Enjoy:**
   - Bring the macarons to room temperature before serving. They can be stored in an airtight container in the refrigerator for up to 5 days, or frozen for longer storage.

Tips for Success:

- **Egg Whites:** Make sure your egg whites are at room temperature for best results.
- **Macaronage:** Folding the batter correctly is crucial. It should flow off the spatula slowly and leave a ribbon that disappears into the batter within about 20 seconds.
- **Resting Time:** This helps develop a smooth top and feet during baking.
- **Consistency:** Aim for a smooth, shiny batter that is not too runny or too stiff.

Enjoy your homemade macarons! They're perfect for special occasions or just as a delightful treat any time.

Tarte Tatin

Ingredients:

For the Pastry:

- 1 1/4 cups (160g) all-purpose flour
- 1/2 tsp salt
- 1/2 tbsp granulated sugar
- 1/2 cup (1 stick or 115g) unsalted butter, cold and cut into small cubes
- 2-3 tbsp ice water

For the Filling:

- 6-7 apples (preferably firm and tart varieties like Granny Smith), peeled, cored, and halved
- 1/2 cup (1 stick or 115g) unsalted butter
- 1 cup (200g) granulated sugar
- 1/4 cup water
- 1 tsp vanilla extract
- Optional: ground cinnamon or nutmeg (to taste)

Instructions:

Making the Pastry:

1. **Prepare the Dough:**
    - In a large bowl, whisk together the flour, salt, and sugar. Add the cold butter cubes and use a pastry cutter or your fingers to work the butter into the flour mixture until it resembles coarse crumbs.
2. **Add Water:**
    - Gradually add ice water, one tablespoon at a time, mixing with a fork until the dough just begins to come together. It should hold together when squeezed with your fingers. Be careful not to overwork the dough.
3. **Form a Disk:**
    - Shape the dough into a disk, wrap it tightly in plastic wrap, and refrigerate for at least 30 minutes (or up to 2 days) to chill.

Making the Tarte Tatin:

1. **Preheat Oven:**
    - Preheat your oven to 375°F (190°C).
2. **Prepare the Caramel:**
    - In a 9 or 10-inch ovenproof skillet (preferably cast iron), melt the butter over medium heat. Add the granulated sugar and water, stirring until the sugar

dissolves. Bring to a simmer and cook until the mixture turns a deep golden caramel color, swirling the pan occasionally to ensure even caramelization.

3. **Arrange Apples:**
    - Remove the skillet from heat and carefully arrange the apple halves, cut side up, in a circular pattern over the caramel. Pack them tightly together as they will shrink while cooking.
4. **Flavoring:**
    - Sprinkle the apples with vanilla extract and optionally with ground cinnamon or nutmeg for extra flavor.
5. **Roll Out the Dough:**
    - On a lightly floured surface, roll out the chilled dough into a circle slightly larger than the skillet.
6. **Assemble and Bake:**
    - Carefully place the rolled-out dough over the apples, tucking in the edges gently around the apples inside the skillet.
7. **Bake:**
    - Bake in the preheated oven for 30-35 minutes, or until the pastry is golden brown and crisp.
8. **Cool and Serve:**
    - Remove the skillet from the oven and let it cool for about 10 minutes. Place a serving plate over the skillet and carefully invert the tart onto the plate. Be cautious as the caramel will be hot.
9. **Serve:**
    - Serve warm, optionally with whipped cream or vanilla ice cream.

Notes:

- **Apples:** Choose firm apples that hold their shape well when baked. Granny Smith apples are traditional for Tarte Tatin due to their tartness and ability to hold up during cooking.
- **Caramel:** Take care when making the caramel as it can become very hot. Use a heavy-bottomed skillet and watch closely to avoid burning.
- **Pastry:** The homemade pastry crust adds a wonderful texture, but you can also use store-bought puff pastry if preferred.

Enjoy your delicious Tarte Tatin, a classic French dessert that's perfect for showcasing seasonal apples!

Madeleines

Ingredients:

- 2/3 cup (130g) granulated sugar
- Zest of 1 lemon (or 1 tsp vanilla extract)
- 3 large eggs, at room temperature
- 1 cup (125g) all-purpose flour
- 1/2 tsp baking powder
- 1/4 tsp salt
- 10 tbsp (140g) unsalted butter, melted and cooled
- Optional: powdered sugar, for dusting

Instructions:

1. **Prepare Madeleine Pan:**
   - Brush the molds of a madeleine pan with melted butter and dust lightly with flour, tapping out any excess. Alternatively, you can use non-stick cooking spray with flour.
2. **Preheat Oven:**
   - Preheat your oven to 375°F (190°C).
3. **Prepare Batter:**
   - In a mixing bowl, combine the sugar and lemon zest (or vanilla extract). Rub the zest into the sugar with your fingers to release the oils and flavor.
4. **Beat Eggs:**
   - Add the eggs to the sugar mixture. Using a hand mixer or stand mixer fitted with the whisk attachment, beat on medium-high speed until the mixture is pale and thick, about 5 minutes.
5. **Sift Dry Ingredients:**
   - In a separate bowl, sift together the flour, baking powder, and salt.
6. **Fold Dry Ingredients:**
   - Gradually fold the dry ingredients into the egg mixture using a spatula, until just combined.
7. **Add Butter:**
   - Gently fold in the melted butter until fully incorporated into the batter.
8. **Fill Madeleine Molds:**
   - Spoon the batter into the prepared madeleine molds, filling each mold about 3/4 full.
9. **Bake:**
   - Bake in the preheated oven for 10-12 minutes, or until the madeleines are puffed up, the edges are golden brown, and the centers spring back when lightly pressed.
10. **Cool and Serve:**

- Remove from the oven and let the madeleines cool in the pan for a few minutes. Then, carefully transfer them to a wire rack to cool completely.

11. **Optional Dusting:**
    - Dust the cooled madeleines with powdered sugar before serving, if desired.

Tips for Success:

- **Room Temperature Eggs:** Ensure your eggs are at room temperature to achieve maximum volume when beating with sugar.
- **Butter:** Melt the butter and allow it to cool slightly before folding it into the batter. This helps maintain the airy texture of the madeleines.
- **Flavor Variations:** Experiment with different flavors such as orange zest, almond extract, or adding chocolate chips for a twist on the classic recipe.
- **Storage:** Madeleines are best enjoyed fresh but can be stored in an airtight container at room temperature for up to 2 days. They can also be frozen for longer storage.

Enjoy your homemade madeleines with a cup of tea or coffee, or serve them as a delightful dessert!

Profiteroles

Ingredients:

For the Choux Pastry:

- 1/2 cup (1 stick) unsalted butter
- 1 cup water
- 1/4 tsp salt
- 1 cup all-purpose flour
- 4 large eggs

For the Filling:

- 1 1/2 cups heavy cream
- 3 tbsp powdered sugar
- 1 tsp vanilla extract

For the Chocolate Ganache:

- 4 oz dark chocolate, chopped
- 1/2 cup heavy cream
- 1 tbsp unsalted butter

Instructions:

Making the Choux Pastry:

1. **Preheat Oven:**
    - Preheat your oven to 400°F (200°C). Line a baking sheet with parchment paper.
2. **Prepare Dough:**
    - In a medium saucepan, combine butter, water, and salt. Bring to a boil over medium heat.
3. **Add Flour:**
    - Reduce heat to low. Add flour all at once, stirring vigorously with a wooden spoon until the mixture forms a ball and pulls away from the sides of the pan. Remove from heat.
4. **Incorporate Eggs:**
    - Transfer the dough to a mixing bowl. Let it cool slightly. Beat in eggs one at a time, mixing well after each addition, until smooth and glossy.
5. **Pipe Dough:**
    - Transfer the dough to a piping bag fitted with a large round tip (or use a resealable plastic bag with a corner cut off). Pipe small mounds (about 1 inch in diameter) onto the prepared baking sheet, leaving space between each for expansion.

6. **Bake:**
   - Bake in the preheated oven for 20-25 minutes or until puffed and golden brown. Pierce each profiterole with a skewer or toothpick to release steam. Cool completely on a wire rack.

Making the Filling:

1. **Whip Cream:**
   - In a mixing bowl, whip the heavy cream, powdered sugar, and vanilla extract until stiff peaks form.
2. **Fill Profiteroles:**
   - Once the profiteroles are completely cooled, cut them in half horizontally using a serrated knife. Spoon or pipe the whipped cream into the bottom half of each profiterole. Replace the top halves.

Making the Chocolate Ganache:

1. **Prepare Ganache:**
   - In a small saucepan, heat the heavy cream until it just begins to boil. Remove from heat and add the chopped chocolate and butter. Let it sit for a minute, then stir until smooth and glossy.
2. **Drizzle Ganache:**
   - Dip the top of each filled profiterole into the chocolate ganache or drizzle the ganache over the profiteroles using a spoon.
3. **Serve:**
   - Arrange the profiteroles on a serving platter. Optionally, dust with powdered sugar before serving.

Notes:

- **Choux Pastry:** Ensure the dough is smooth and glossy before piping. The profiteroles should puff up nicely and have a hollow center to fill with cream.
- **Filling Variations:** Besides whipped cream, you can also fill profiteroles with pastry cream, ice cream, or a flavored whipped cream.
- **Chocolate Ganache:** Adjust the thickness of the ganache by adding more cream for a thinner consistency or more chocolate for a thicker glaze.

Enjoy your homemade profiteroles as a delightful dessert or treat! They are perfect for special occasions and can be enjoyed with coffee or tea.

Palmiers

Ingredients:

- 1 sheet of puff pastry (store-bought or homemade)
- 1/2 cup granulated sugar
- Optional: 1/2 tsp ground cinnamon (for cinnamon palmiers)

Instructions:

1. **Preheat Oven:**
    - Preheat your oven to 400°F (200°C). Line a baking sheet with parchment paper.
2. **Prepare Puff Pastry:**
    - If using store-bought puff pastry, thaw it according to package instructions. If making homemade puff pastry, roll it out into a rectangle about 1/8 inch thick.
3. **Sprinkle Sugar:**
    - Sprinkle half of the granulated sugar evenly over your work surface. Place the puff pastry sheet on top of the sugar.
4. **Sprinkle More Sugar:**
    - Sprinkle the remaining granulated sugar over the puff pastry sheet. Optionally, sprinkle ground cinnamon evenly over the sugar for cinnamon palmiers.
5. **Fold Puff Pastry:**
    - Starting from one of the shorter sides, carefully fold the puff pastry towards the center, stopping when you reach the middle. Repeat from the other side so both sides meet in the center, resembling a double fold.
6. **Fold Again:**
    - Fold the pastry again along the centerline to create a double fold, resulting in a long, narrow strip.
7. **Slice Palmiers:**
    - Using a sharp knife, slice the pastry crosswise into 1/2 inch slices.
8. **Shape Palmiers:**
    - Take each slice and gently press down with your palm to slightly flatten and spread out. Arrange them on the prepared baking sheet, leaving space between each for expansion.
9. **Bake:**
    - Bake in the preheated oven for 15-18 minutes, or until the palmiers are golden brown and crispy, flipping them over halfway through baking to ensure even caramelization.
10. **Cool and Serve:**
    - Remove from the oven and let cool on a wire rack. Once cooled, serve and enjoy these delicious palmiers!

Tips for Success:

- **Sugar Caramelization:** Ensure the sugar is evenly distributed over the puff pastry to achieve a crisp and caramelized exterior.
- **Even Slicing:** Use a sharp knife to ensure clean cuts when slicing the pastry. This helps in creating evenly shaped palmiers.
- **Variations:** Besides cinnamon, you can experiment with other flavors such as cocoa powder, citrus zest, or even a sprinkle of sea salt for a savory twist.

Palmiers are a wonderful treat that pairs perfectly with coffee or tea. They are also great for parties or as a homemade gift. Enjoy making and indulging in these crispy, caramelized delights!

Mille-feuille

Ingredients:

For the Puff Pastry:

- 1 sheet of puff pastry (store-bought or homemade)

For the Pastry Cream:

- 2 cups whole milk
- 1/2 cup granulated sugar
- 4 large egg yolks
- 1/4 cup cornstarch
- 1 tsp vanilla extract

For Assembly:

- Powdered sugar, for dusting
- Optional: icing or fondant for decoration

Instructions:

Making the Puff Pastry:

1. **Preheat Oven:**
    - Preheat your oven to 400°F (200°C). Line a baking sheet with parchment paper.
2. **Prepare Puff Pastry:**
    - If using store-bought puff pastry, thaw it according to package instructions. If making homemade puff pastry, roll it out into a rectangle about 1/8 inch thick. Prick the pastry sheet all over with a fork to prevent excessive puffing.
3. **Bake Puff Pastry:**
    - Place the prepared puff pastry sheet on the baking sheet. Bake in the preheated oven for 15-20 minutes or until golden brown and puffed. Remove from the oven and let it cool completely on a wire rack.

Making the Pastry Cream:

1. **Heat Milk:**
    - In a medium saucepan, heat the milk over medium heat until it just begins to boil. Remove from heat.
2. **Mix Egg Yolks and Sugar:**
    - In a mixing bowl, whisk together the sugar, egg yolks, and cornstarch until smooth and pale.
3. **Temper and Cook:**

- Gradually whisk the hot milk into the egg yolk mixture. Pour the mixture back into the saucepan and cook over medium heat, stirring constantly, until it thickens and comes to a boil.
4. **Flavor:**
    - Remove from heat and stir in the vanilla extract. Transfer to a bowl and cover with plastic wrap directly on the surface to prevent a skin from forming. Chill in the refrigerator until cold.

Assembling the Mille-feuille:

1. **Prepare Puff Pastry Layers:**
    - Once the puff pastry is completely cooled, trim the edges to make straight edges. Cut the pastry into three equal rectangular pieces.
2. **Layering:**
    - Place one piece of puff pastry on a serving platter or plate. Spread a generous layer of chilled pastry cream evenly over the pastry. Top with another piece of puff pastry and another layer of pastry cream. Finish with the third piece of puff pastry on top.
3. **Decoration:**
    - Dust the top layer of puff pastry with powdered sugar. Optionally, you can drizzle icing or decorate with fondant.
4. **Chill and Serve:**
    - Refrigerate the assembled mille-feuille for at least 1 hour before serving to allow the layers to set. Slice into portions and serve chilled.

Notes:

- **Puff Pastry:** Using good quality puff pastry is important for achieving light and flaky layers. If making homemade puff pastry, ensure it's well chilled and handled gently to preserve the layers.
- **Pastry Cream:** Make sure the pastry cream is chilled before assembling the mille-feuille to prevent it from melting the layers.
- **Variations:** You can add fresh berries or a layer of jam between the pastry cream layers for added flavor and texture.

Enjoy your homemade mille-feuille! It's a beautiful and elegant dessert that will impress your guests or make any occasion special.

Choux à la Crème (Cream Puffs)

Ingredients:

For the Choux Pastry:

- 1/2 cup water
- 1/2 cup milk
- 1/2 cup unsalted butter, cut into cubes
- 1 tablespoon granulated sugar
- 1/4 teaspoon salt
- 1 cup all-purpose flour
- 4 large eggs

For the Pastry Cream:

- 1 cup whole milk
- 1/2 vanilla bean, split and seeds scraped out (or 1 teaspoon vanilla extract)
- 3 large egg yolks
- 1/4 cup granulated sugar
- 2 tablespoons cornstarch
- Pinch of salt
- 2 tablespoons unsalted butter

For Assembly:

- Powdered sugar, for dusting

Instructions:

1. Make the Choux Pastry:

- Preheat your oven to 400°F (200°C). Line a baking sheet with parchment paper or silicone mat.
- In a medium saucepan, combine water, milk, butter, sugar, and salt. Bring to a boil over medium heat.
- Once boiling, add the flour all at once. Stir vigorously with a wooden spoon until the mixture forms a ball and pulls away from the sides of the pan.
- Transfer the dough to a mixing bowl and let it cool slightly for about 5 minutes.
- Using a hand mixer or a stand mixer fitted with a paddle attachment, beat in the eggs one at a time, mixing well after each addition, until you have a smooth, shiny dough.

2. Shape and Bake the Choux:

- Transfer the choux pastry dough to a piping bag fitted with a large round tip (or you can use a spoon). Pipe mounds onto the prepared baking sheet, leaving space between each for expansion.
- Bake in the preheated oven for 15 minutes, then reduce the oven temperature to 350°F (180°C) and bake for an additional 20-25 minutes, or until the choux are golden brown and crisp. Do not open the oven door during the first 15 minutes of baking to prevent the puffs from deflating.
- Remove from the oven and let cool completely on a wire rack.

3. Make the Pastry Cream:

- In a saucepan, heat the milk and vanilla bean (or vanilla extract) over medium heat until just simmering. Remove from heat and let steep for 10-15 minutes.
- In a medium bowl, whisk together the egg yolks, sugar, cornstarch, and salt until pale and thick.
- Gradually pour the warm milk into the egg mixture, whisking constantly.
- Return the mixture to the saucepan and cook over medium heat, whisking constantly, until thickened and large bubbles start to appear.
- Remove from heat and stir in the butter until smooth. Strain the pastry cream through a fine-mesh sieve into a clean bowl.
- Cover the surface of the pastry cream with plastic wrap (to prevent a skin from forming) and chill in the refrigerator until cold.

4. Assemble the Choux à la Crème:

- Once the choux puffs are completely cooled, use a small knife to make a small slit on the side of each puff.
- Transfer the chilled pastry cream to a piping bag fitted with a small round tip (or you can use a spoon). Pipe the pastry cream into each puff until filled.
- Dust the filled puffs with powdered sugar before serving.

Enjoy your homemade Choux à la Crème! These delightful cream puffs are best served fresh, but you can store any leftovers in an airtight container in the refrigerator for up to 2 days.

Financiers

Ingredients:

- 1 cup (225g) unsalted butter
- 1 cup (100g) almond flour (ground almonds)
- 1 cup (120g) powdered sugar
- 1/2 cup (60g) all-purpose flour
- 1/4 teaspoon salt
- 6 large egg whites
- 1 teaspoon vanilla extract
- Optional: Sliced almonds or whole almonds for decoration

Instructions:

1. Brown the Butter:

- Cut the butter into pieces and place it in a small saucepan over medium heat.
- Cook the butter, stirring occasionally, until it foams and then turns a deep golden brown color. This process will take about 5-7 minutes. Be careful not to burn the butter.
- Once browned, immediately remove from heat and pour into a heatproof bowl. Let it cool to room temperature.

2. Prepare the Financier Batter:

- Preheat your oven to 375°F (190°C). Grease or line a financier mold or mini muffin tin.
- In a large bowl, whisk together the almond flour, powdered sugar, all-purpose flour, and salt.
- In another bowl, lightly whisk the egg whites until just frothy (do not whip).
- Pour the egg whites into the dry ingredients and stir until just combined.
- Gently fold in the cooled brown butter and vanilla extract until you have a smooth batter.

3. Bake the Financiers:

- Fill each mold of the financier pan or mini muffin tin about 3/4 full with the batter.
- If desired, place a sliced almond or whole almond on top of each financier for decoration.
- Bake in the preheated oven for 12-15 minutes, or until the financiers are golden brown around the edges and a toothpick inserted into the center comes out clean.
- Remove from the oven and let cool in the pan for a few minutes, then transfer to a wire rack to cool completely.

4. Serve:

- Once cooled, dust with powdered sugar if desired.
- Financiers can be stored in an airtight container at room temperature for up to 3 days.

Enjoy these delicious almond cakes with a cup of tea or coffee! They make a perfect treat for any occasion.

Pâte à Choux

Ingredients:

- 1/2 cup (120ml) water
- 1/2 cup (120ml) whole milk
- 1/2 cup (113g) unsalted butter, cut into small pieces
- 1 tablespoon granulated sugar
- 1/4 teaspoon salt
- 1 cup (125g) all-purpose flour
- 4 large eggs, at room temperature

Instructions:

1. Prepare the Dough:

- Preheat your oven to 400°F (200°C). Line a baking sheet with parchment paper or a silicone mat.
- In a medium saucepan, combine water, milk, butter, sugar, and salt. Place over medium heat and bring to a simmer, stirring occasionally.
- Once the mixture is simmering and the butter has melted completely, reduce the heat to low and add all the flour at once.
- Stir vigorously with a wooden spoon or spatula until the mixture comes together into a smooth dough and pulls away from the sides of the pan. This should take about 1-2 minutes.

2. Cook the Dough:

- Continue to cook the dough over low heat, stirring constantly, for another 1-2 minutes. This helps to dry out the dough slightly and cook off excess moisture.
- Transfer the dough to the bowl of a stand mixer fitted with a paddle attachment, or you can use a hand mixer.
- Let the dough cool for a few minutes to avoid cooking the eggs when added next.

3. Add Eggs:

- Beat the eggs in a separate bowl. Add them to the dough one at a time, mixing well after each addition. The dough may initially appear lumpy or separated after adding each egg, but it will come together into a smooth, glossy, and thick paste by the time all eggs are fully incorporated.
- The dough should be smooth and glossy, and when you lift the paddle or beaters, it should fall back into the bowl in a thick ribbon.

4. Pipe and Bake:

- Transfer the Pâte à Choux dough to a piping bag fitted with a large round tip (or use a spoon).
- Pipe the dough onto the prepared baking sheet into the desired shapes. For cream puffs or éclairs, pipe mounds or logs that are about 1.5 inches (4 cm) in diameter and 2 inches (5 cm) apart.
- Optionally, you can brush the tops with a beaten egg wash for a shiny finish.
- Bake in the preheated oven for 15 minutes, then reduce the oven temperature to 350°F (180°C) and bake for an additional 20-25 minutes, or until the Pâte à Choux is golden brown and crisp.

5. Cool and Fill:

- Remove from the oven and let the Pâte à Choux cool completely on a wire rack.
- Once cooled, you can fill the Pâte à Choux with sweetened whipped cream, pastry cream, or savory fillings like cheese or mousse.

Tips:

- **Consistency Check:** The dough should be thick enough to hold its shape when piped but soft enough to be piped smoothly.
- **Avoid Opening the Oven:** During baking, avoid opening the oven door too often as it can cause the Pâte à Choux to collapse.
- **Storage:** Pâte à Choux pastries are best enjoyed fresh but can be stored unfilled in an airtight container at room temperature for a day or two. Filled pastries should be refrigerated and consumed within a day for best taste and texture.

Enjoy making and serving these delightful French pastries!

Cannele

Ingredients:

- 2 cups (500ml) whole milk
- 2 tablespoons (30g) unsalted butter
- 1 cup (200g) granulated sugar
- 1 cup (125g) all-purpose flour
- 4 large egg yolks
- 2 large eggs
- 1/4 teaspoon salt
- 2 tablespoons (30ml) dark rum (optional)
- 1 teaspoon vanilla extract
- Butter and beeswax or butter and cooking spray for greasing molds

Instructions:

1. Prepare the Batter:

- In a saucepan, combine the milk and butter. Heat over medium heat until the butter is melted and the mixture is hot but not boiling. Remove from heat and let it cool slightly.
- In a large bowl, whisk together the sugar, flour, egg yolks, eggs, and salt until smooth and well combined.
- Gradually pour the warm milk mixture into the egg mixture, whisking constantly until smooth.
- Stir in the rum (if using) and vanilla extract. Cover the batter and refrigerate for at least 12 hours, or up to 48 hours. This resting period allows the flavors to develop and ensures a better texture.

2. Prepare the Molds:

- Before baking, prepare your cannele molds. Traditional cannele molds are made of copper and should be buttered and lined with beeswax for a better caramelization and release. However, silicone molds or well-buttered metal molds can also be used.

3. Bake the Cannele:

- Preheat your oven to 450°F (230°C).
- Stir the batter gently to reincorporate any settled ingredients.
- Fill each mold almost to the top with the batter.
- Place the molds on a baking sheet and bake in the preheated oven for 10 minutes.
- Reduce the oven temperature to 375°F (190°C) and continue baking for another 50-60 minutes, or until the canneles are dark brown and caramelized on the outside.
- Remove from the oven and let cool in the molds for 10 minutes.

4. Unmold and Serve:

- Gently loosen the canneles from the molds using a knife or silicone spatula.
- Transfer the canneles to a wire rack to cool completely before serving.

5. Enjoy:

- Canneles are best enjoyed the day they are made when the exterior is crisp and caramelized, and the interior is soft and custardy. They can be stored in an airtight container at room temperature for a day or two, but their texture may change over time.

Tips:

- **Molds:** If using copper molds, make sure to properly butter and line them with beeswax. If using silicone molds or metal molds, ensure they are well-greased to prevent sticking.
- **Batter Consistency:** The batter should be refrigerated for at least 12 hours to allow the flavors to develop and the flour to hydrate fully.
- **Baking Time:** Baking times may vary depending on your oven and the size of your molds. Adjust accordingly to achieve the desired caramelization on the outside while ensuring the inside remains custardy.

Enjoy these delightful canneles with a cup of coffee or tea for a true taste of French pastry perfection!

Brioche

Ingredients:

- 4 cups (500g) all-purpose flour
- 1/4 cup (50g) granulated sugar
- 2 teaspoons active dry yeast
- 1 teaspoon salt
- 4 large eggs, at room temperature
- 1/2 cup (120ml) warm milk
- 1 cup (225g) unsalted butter, softened and cut into pieces, plus extra for greasing
- 1 egg yolk, beaten (for egg wash)

Instructions:

1. Prepare the Dough:

- In a large mixing bowl or the bowl of a stand mixer fitted with a dough hook, combine the flour, sugar, yeast, and salt.
- Make a well in the center and add the eggs and warm milk. Mix gently with a wooden spoon or on low speed until the dough starts to come together.
- Continue mixing while gradually adding the softened butter, piece by piece, until it is all incorporated and the dough is smooth and elastic. This may take about 10-15 minutes of kneading with a mixer or longer by hand.

2. First Rise:

- Once the dough is smooth and elastic, shape it into a ball and place it in a lightly greased bowl. Cover with plastic wrap or a clean kitchen towel and let it rise in a warm, draft-free place until doubled in size, about 1-2 hours.

3. Shape the Brioche:

- After the dough has doubled in size, gently punch it down to release the air.
- Divide the dough into equal portions and shape them into desired shapes. Brioche can be shaped into loaves, buns, or even made into braids.
- Place the shaped dough on a baking sheet lined with parchment paper or greased with butter. Cover loosely with plastic wrap or a kitchen towel.

4. Second Rise:

- Let the shaped dough rise again in a warm place until doubled in size, about 1 hour.

5. Bake the Brioche:

- Preheat your oven to 375°F (190°C).

- Brush the tops of the brioche with beaten egg yolk for a shiny finish.
- Bake in the preheated oven for 20-25 minutes, or until the brioche is golden brown and sounds hollow when tapped on the bottom.
- If baking larger loaves, they may need additional time. Cover with foil if they start to brown too quickly.

6. Cool and Enjoy:

- Remove the brioche from the oven and let cool on a wire rack.
- Serve the brioche warm or at room temperature. It's delicious on its own, with butter and jam, or as the base for French toast.

Tips:

- **Room Temperature Ingredients:** Ensure your eggs and butter are at room temperature before starting to help the dough come together smoothly.
- **Rising Times:** Rising times can vary depending on the temperature of your kitchen. Be patient and allow the dough to rise until doubled in size at each stage.
- **Variations:** Brioche can be flavored with additions like orange zest, cinnamon, or chocolate chips for different variations.

Enjoy your homemade brioche! It's a delightful treat that's perfect for breakfast, brunch, or anytime you crave a delicious, buttery bread.

Pain de Campagne (French Country Bread)

Ingredients:

- 2 cups (250g) bread flour
- 1 cup (125g) whole wheat flour
- 1 1/2 teaspoons salt
- 1 1/4 teaspoons active dry yeast (or 1 teaspoon instant yeast)
- 1 1/4 cups (300ml) lukewarm water
- Optional: 1 tablespoon honey or sugar (for a touch of sweetness, if desired)

Instructions:

1. Mix the Dough:

- In a large mixing bowl, combine the bread flour, whole wheat flour, salt, and yeast. If using honey or sugar, add it to the lukewarm water and stir until dissolved.
- Gradually add the lukewarm water to the flour mixture, stirring with a wooden spoon or spatula until a rough dough forms.

2. Knead the Dough:

- Turn the dough out onto a lightly floured surface. Knead the dough for about 10 minutes until it becomes smooth and elastic. Alternatively, you can knead the dough with a stand mixer fitted with a dough hook for about 8-10 minutes on medium speed.
- The dough should be slightly tacky but not sticky. Add a little more flour or water as needed to achieve the right consistency.

3. First Rise:

- Place the dough in a lightly greased bowl, cover with plastic wrap or a kitchen towel, and let it rise in a warm, draft-free place until doubled in size, about 1-2 hours.

4. Shape the Loaf:

- Once doubled in size, gently deflate the dough and shape it into a round or oval loaf. You can do this by folding the dough over itself a few times, then shaping it into a smooth ball or log.
- Place the shaped dough on a parchment-lined baking sheet or a floured proofing basket (banneton).

5. Second Rise:

- Cover the shaped dough loosely with plastic wrap or a kitchen towel and let it rise again until puffy and almost doubled in size, about 1 hour.

6. Preheat the Oven:

- About 30 minutes before baking, preheat your oven to 450°F (230°C). Place a baking stone or an inverted baking sheet on the middle rack of the oven.

7. Score and Bake:

- If using a proofing basket, gently invert the dough onto a parchment-lined baking sheet. Using a sharp knife or bread lame, score the top of the loaf with 1-2 slashes.
- Transfer the loaf (or baking sheet) to the preheated baking stone or inverted baking sheet in the oven.
- Bake for 25-30 minutes, or until the bread is golden brown and sounds hollow when tapped on the bottom.
- If you prefer a softer crust, you can bake at 400°F (200°C) for a longer time.

8. Cool and Enjoy:

- Remove the bread from the oven and let it cool on a wire rack for at least 30 minutes before slicing.

Tips:

- **Flour Variations:** You can adjust the ratio of bread flour to whole wheat flour based on your preference. A higher proportion of whole wheat flour will result in a denser loaf with a stronger wheat flavor.
- **Water Temperature:** Lukewarm water should be around 100-110°F (37-43°C) to activate the yeast properly without killing it.
- **Baking Stone:** Using a baking stone or inverted baking sheet helps create a crisp crust by evenly distributing heat.
- **Storage:** Store the cooled bread in a paper bag or bread box to maintain its crust. It's best enjoyed fresh, but you can also freeze slices for longer storage.

Enjoy your homemade Pain de Campagne! It's perfect for sandwiches, toasts, or simply with a spread of butter.

Quiche Lorraine

Ingredients:

For the Pastry Crust:

- 1 1/4 cups (160g) all-purpose flour
- 1/2 teaspoon salt
- 1/2 cup (115g) unsalted butter, cold and cut into cubes
- 3-4 tablespoons ice water

For the Filling:

- 8 oz (225g) bacon, diced
- 1 cup (240ml) heavy cream
- 1 cup (240ml) milk
- 4 large eggs
- 1/4 teaspoon salt
- 1/4 teaspoon black pepper
- Pinch of nutmeg (optional)
- 1 cup (100g) shredded Gruyère cheese (or Swiss cheese)
- Optional: Chopped fresh chives or parsley for garnish

Instructions:

1. Make the Pastry Crust:

- In a food processor, combine the flour and salt. Add the cold butter cubes and pulse until the mixture resembles coarse crumbs.
- Add the ice water, 1 tablespoon at a time, pulsing until the dough just begins to come together. Be careful not to overwork the dough.
- Turn the dough out onto a lightly floured surface and gather into a ball. Flatten into a disk, wrap in plastic wrap, and refrigerate for at least 1 hour, or up to 2 days.

2. Prepare the Filling:

- In a skillet over medium heat, cook the diced bacon until crispy. Remove from the skillet and drain on paper towels.
- In a bowl, whisk together the heavy cream, milk, eggs, salt, pepper, and nutmeg (if using) until well combined.

3. Prebake the Pastry Crust:

- Preheat your oven to 375°F (190°C).
- On a lightly floured surface, roll out the chilled pastry dough into a circle about 12 inches (30cm) in diameter.

- Carefully transfer the dough to a 9-inch (23cm) tart pan with a removable bottom. Press the dough into the bottom and sides of the pan. Trim any excess dough.
- Line the pastry crust with parchment paper or aluminum foil and fill with pie weights or dried beans.
- Bake in the preheated oven for 15 minutes. Remove the weights and parchment/foil, then bake for an additional 5 minutes until the crust is lightly golden. Remove from the oven and let cool slightly.

4. Assemble and Bake the Quiche:

- Sprinkle the shredded cheese evenly over the bottom of the partially baked pastry crust.
- Scatter the cooked bacon over the cheese.
- Pour the egg and cream mixture evenly over the bacon and cheese.
- Reduce the oven temperature to 350°F (175°C) and bake the quiche for 30-35 minutes, or until the filling is set and the top is lightly golden brown.

5. Serve:

- Remove the quiche from the oven and let it cool in the tart pan for a few minutes.
- Carefully remove the quiche from the tart pan and transfer to a serving plate.
- Garnish with chopped fresh chives or parsley if desired.

6. Enjoy:

- Serve the Quiche Lorraine warm or at room temperature, cut into wedges.

Tips:

- **Make Ahead:** You can prepare the pastry dough and refrigerate it for up to 2 days before rolling it out and baking.
- **Variations:** Feel free to customize your quiche by adding onions, mushrooms, or different types of cheeses.
- **Storage:** Leftover quiche can be stored in the refrigerator for up to 3 days. Reheat gently in the oven or microwave before serving.

Quiche Lorraine makes for a delicious brunch or lunch dish, paired with a green salad or served on its own. Enjoy this classic French savory tart!

Galettes des Rois (King Cake)

Ingredients:

For the Pastry Crust:

- 1 1/4 cups (160g) all-purpose flour
- 1/2 teaspoon salt
- 1/2 cup (115g) unsalted butter, cold and cut into cubes
- 3-4 tablespoons ice water

For the Filling:

- 8 oz (225g) bacon, diced
- 1 cup (240ml) heavy cream
- 1 cup (240ml) milk
- 4 large eggs
- 1/4 teaspoon salt
- 1/4 teaspoon black pepper
- Pinch of nutmeg (optional)
- 1 cup (100g) shredded Gruyère cheese (or Swiss cheese)
- Optional: Chopped fresh chives or parsley for garnish

Instructions:

1. Make the Pastry Crust:

- In a food processor, combine the flour and salt. Add the cold butter cubes and pulse until the mixture resembles coarse crumbs.
- Add the ice water, 1 tablespoon at a time, pulsing until the dough just begins to come together. Be careful not to overwork the dough.
- Turn the dough out onto a lightly floured surface and gather into a ball. Flatten into a disk, wrap in plastic wrap, and refrigerate for at least 1 hour, or up to 2 days.

2. Prepare the Filling:

- In a skillet over medium heat, cook the diced bacon until crispy. Remove from the skillet and drain on paper towels.
- In a bowl, whisk together the heavy cream, milk, eggs, salt, pepper, and nutmeg (if using) until well combined.

3. Prebake the Pastry Crust:

- Preheat your oven to 375°F (190°C).
- On a lightly floured surface, roll out the chilled pastry dough into a circle about 12 inches (30cm) in diameter.

- Carefully transfer the dough to a 9-inch (23cm) tart pan with a removable bottom. Press the dough into the bottom and sides of the pan. Trim any excess dough.
- Line the pastry crust with parchment paper or aluminum foil and fill with pie weights or dried beans.
- Bake in the preheated oven for 15 minutes. Remove the weights and parchment/foil, then bake for an additional 5 minutes until the crust is lightly golden. Remove from the oven and let cool slightly.

4. Assemble and Bake the Quiche:

- Sprinkle the shredded cheese evenly over the bottom of the partially baked pastry crust.
- Scatter the cooked bacon over the cheese.
- Pour the egg and cream mixture evenly over the bacon and cheese.
- Reduce the oven temperature to 350°F (175°C) and bake the quiche for 30-35 minutes, or until the filling is set and the top is lightly golden brown.

5. Serve:

- Remove the quiche from the oven and let it cool in the tart pan for a few minutes.
- Carefully remove the quiche from the tart pan and transfer to a serving plate.
- Garnish with chopped fresh chives or parsley if desired.

6. Enjoy:

- Serve the Quiche Lorraine warm or at room temperature, cut into wedges.

Tips:

- **Make Ahead:** You can prepare the pastry dough and refrigerate it for up to 2 days before rolling it out and baking.
- **Variations:** Feel free to customize your quiche by adding onions, mushrooms, or different types of cheeses.
- **Storage:** Leftover quiche can be stored in the refrigerator for up to 3 days. Reheat gently in the oven or microwave before serving.

Quiche Lorraine makes for a delicious brunch or lunch dish, paired with a green salad or served on its own. Enjoy this classic French savory tart!

Galettes des Rois (King Cake)

Ingredients:

For the Frangipane Filling:

- 1 cup (100g) almond flour
- 1/2 cup (100g) granulated sugar
- 1/2 cup (115g) unsalted butter, softened
- 2 large eggs
- 1 tablespoon all-purpose flour
- 1 teaspoon vanilla extract
- 1/2 teaspoon almond extract (optional)
- 1/4 teaspoon salt

For the Galette:

- 2 sheets of puff pastry (store-bought or homemade), thawed if frozen
- 1 egg yolk, beaten (for egg wash)
- Optional: 1 fève or small figurine

Instructions:

1. Prepare the Frangipane Filling:

- In a medium bowl, cream together the softened butter and granulated sugar until light and fluffy.
- Add the almond flour, all-purpose flour, salt, vanilla extract, and almond extract (if using). Mix until well combined.
- Beat in the eggs, one at a time, until smooth and creamy. Set aside.

2. Assemble the Galette des Rois:

- Preheat your oven to 400°F (200°C). Line a baking sheet with parchment paper.
- Roll out one sheet of puff pastry on a lightly floured surface into a circle or rectangle, depending on the shape you prefer (traditionally, it's round).
- Transfer the rolled-out pastry to the prepared baking sheet.
- Spread the frangipane filling evenly over the center of the pastry, leaving a border of about 1 inch (2.5 cm) around the edges.
- If using, place the fève or small figurine somewhere in the frangipane filling (be sure to warn your guests before serving).
- Brush the edges of the pastry with water to help seal the galette.
- Place the second sheet of puff pastry on top of the filling. Press the edges firmly together to seal.
- Trim any excess pastry if necessary, and crimp the edges with a fork to seal completely.

3. Bake the Galette des Rois:

- Brush the top of the galette with beaten egg yolk for a shiny finish.
- Use a sharp knife to make decorative patterns or slashes on the top of the galette, being careful not to cut all the way through.
- Bake in the preheated oven for 25-30 minutes, or until the galette is golden brown and puffed up.

4. Serve:

- Remove from the oven and let the galette cool slightly on a wire rack before serving.
- Traditionally, Galette des Rois is served at room temperature. It's customary to crown the youngest person present with a paper crown (often provided with the galette) and slice the galette into portions to see who finds the fève.

Tips:

- **Puff Pastry:** If using store-bought puff pastry, ensure it is thawed according to package instructions before using.
- **Frangipane Variation:** You can also make a different filling with pastry cream (crème pâtissière) or fruit compote for a variation.
- **Storage:** Galette des Rois is best enjoyed freshly baked. Any leftovers can be stored in an airtight container in the refrigerator for up to 2 days.

Enjoy this delightful French tradition of Galette des Rois, celebrating the Epiphany with family and friends!

Clafoutis

Ingredients:

- 1 tablespoon unsalted butter, for greasing the baking dish
- 1 cup (150g) fresh cherries, pitted (or any other fruit of your choice, such as berries, peaches, or plums)
- 3 large eggs
- 1/2 cup (100g) granulated sugar
- 1 cup (240ml) whole milk
- 1/2 cup (120ml) heavy cream
- 1 teaspoon vanilla extract
- Pinch of salt
- 1/2 cup (60g) all-purpose flour
- Powdered sugar, for dusting (optional)

Instructions:

1. Prepare the Baking Dish:

- Preheat your oven to 350°F (175°C). Grease a 9-inch (23cm) round baking dish (or a similar size) with butter.

2. Prepare the Fruit:

- Wash and pit the cherries (or prepare your choice of fruit). Spread them evenly in the greased baking dish.

3. Make the Batter:

- In a large bowl, whisk together the eggs and granulated sugar until well combined and slightly frothy.
- Add the whole milk, heavy cream, vanilla extract, and pinch of salt. Whisk until smooth.
- Gradually whisk in the all-purpose flour until the batter is smooth and there are no lumps.

4. Assemble and Bake:

- Pour the batter evenly over the fruit in the baking dish. The fruit may float to the top, which is normal.
- Place the baking dish in the preheated oven and bake for 35-40 minutes, or until the clafoutis is puffed up and golden brown on top. It should be set in the center but still slightly jiggly.

5. Serve:

- Remove from the oven and let cool slightly on a wire rack. The clafoutis will deflate a bit as it cools.
- Dust with powdered sugar before serving, if desired.

6. Enjoy:

- Serve the clafoutis warm or at room temperature. It can be enjoyed on its own or with a dollop of whipped cream or a scoop of vanilla ice cream.

Tips:

- **Fruit Variations:** While cherries are traditional, feel free to experiment with other fruits like berries, sliced peaches, plums, or even apples.
- **Batter Consistency:** The batter should be thin and pourable but not too watery. It should coat the back of a spoon.
- **Pitting Cherries:** If using cherries, you can pit them using a cherry pitter or carefully with a knife.
- **Storage:** Clafoutis is best enjoyed fresh on the day it's made. Leftovers can be stored covered in the refrigerator and gently reheated in the oven before serving.

Clafoutis makes for a delightful and comforting dessert, perfect for showcasing seasonal fruits. Enjoy this classic French treat with your favorite fruits and a touch of powdered sugar!

Soufflé

Ingredients:

- 2 tablespoons unsalted butter, plus extra for greasing the ramekins
- 1/4 cup (30g) grated Parmesan cheese, for coating the ramekins
- 3 tablespoons all-purpose flour
- 1 cup (240ml) whole milk
- 1 cup (100g) grated Gruyère cheese (or any other cheese of your choice)
- 4 large eggs, separated
- Salt and pepper, to taste
- Pinch of cayenne pepper (optional)
- Pinch of nutmeg (optional)

Instructions:

1. Prepare the Ramekins:

- Preheat your oven to 375°F (190°C). Butter the inside of four 8-ounce (250ml) ramekins thoroughly. Coat the buttered ramekins with grated Parmesan cheese, shaking out any excess. This helps the soufflé to rise properly.

2. Make the Base:

- In a medium saucepan, melt the butter over medium heat. Stir in the flour and cook for about 1 minute, stirring constantly, until the mixture is smooth and bubbly.
- Gradually whisk in the milk, stirring constantly until the mixture thickens and comes to a boil. Cook for another minute until smooth and thickened.
- Remove from heat and stir in the grated Gruyère cheese until melted. Season with salt, pepper, cayenne pepper (if using), and nutmeg (if using). Let the mixture cool slightly.

3. Prepare the Egg Yolks:

- Separate the eggs, placing the yolks in a small bowl. Beat the egg yolks lightly with a fork.
- Gradually whisk the beaten egg yolks into the cheese mixture until well combined. Set aside.

4. Whip the Egg Whites:

- In a clean, dry bowl, using a hand mixer or a stand mixer fitted with the whisk attachment, beat the egg whites on medium-high speed until stiff peaks form. This will take a few minutes.

5. Combine and Fold:

- Gently fold about one-third of the whipped egg whites into the cheese mixture to lighten it. Then, carefully fold in the remaining egg whites until just combined. Be gentle to preserve the airiness of the egg whites.

6. Bake the Soufflés:

- Spoon the soufflé mixture into the prepared ramekins, filling each almost to the top. Smooth the tops with a spatula.
- Place the filled ramekins on a baking sheet and immediately transfer to the preheated oven.
- Bake for 18-20 minutes, or until the soufflés are puffed up and golden brown on top. Do not open the oven door during baking to prevent the soufflés from deflating.

7. Serve Immediately:

- Carefully remove the soufflés from the oven and serve immediately while they are hot and puffy.

Tips:

- **Ramekins:** Using properly prepared ramekins (buttered and coated with cheese) helps the soufflé to climb up the sides as it bakes.
- **Egg Whites:** Make sure your egg whites are beaten to stiff peaks for the best volume and structure.
- **Seasoning:** Adjust the seasoning according to your taste preferences. You can add herbs, spices, or other cheeses to customize the flavor of your soufflé.
- **Timing:** Soufflés are best served immediately after baking as they will begin to deflate shortly after being removed from the oven. However, they are still delicious even as they deflate.

Enjoy the light and fluffy texture of your homemade cheese soufflé as a delightful appetizer or main dish paired with a salad! Adjust the recipe for sweet soufflés by omitting the cheese and adding sugar and flavorings such as chocolate or fruit purée.

Tarte au Citron (Lemon Tart)

Ingredients:

For the Tart Crust:

- 1 1/4 cups (160g) all-purpose flour
- 1/3 cup (40g) powdered sugar
- 1/4 teaspoon salt
- 1/2 cup (115g) unsalted butter, cold and cut into cubes
- 1 large egg yolk
- 1-2 tablespoons ice water, if needed

For the Lemon Filling:

- 4-5 large lemons (you will need 1 cup (240ml) of lemon juice and the zest of 2 lemons)
- 1 cup (200g) granulated sugar
- 4 large eggs
- 1/2 cup (120ml) heavy cream
- Pinch of salt
- 1/4 cup (60g) unsalted butter, cubed

Instructions:

1. Make the Tart Crust:

- In a food processor, combine the flour, powdered sugar, and salt. Pulse a few times to mix.
- Add the cold butter cubes and pulse until the mixture resembles coarse crumbs.
- Add the egg yolk and pulse until the dough starts to come together. If the dough seems too dry, add 1-2 tablespoons of ice water, pulsing until the dough forms clumps.
- Turn the dough out onto a lightly floured surface and gather into a ball. Flatten into a disk, wrap in plastic wrap, and refrigerate for at least 30 minutes.
- Preheat your oven to 375°F (190°C).
- On a lightly floured surface, roll out the chilled dough into a circle about 12 inches (30cm) in diameter. Carefully transfer the dough to a 9-inch (23cm) tart pan with a removable bottom. Press the dough into the bottom and sides of the pan. Trim any excess dough.
- Prick the bottom of the tart crust with a fork. Line the crust with parchment paper or aluminum foil and fill with pie weights or dried beans.
- Bake in the preheated oven for 15 minutes. Remove the weights and parchment/foil, then bake for an additional 5-7 minutes until the crust is golden brown. Remove from the oven and let cool slightly.

2. Make the Lemon Filling:

- While the crust is baking, prepare the lemon filling. Zest 2 lemons and squeeze enough lemons to yield 1 cup (240ml) of lemon juice.
- In a heatproof bowl, whisk together the granulated sugar, eggs, lemon juice, lemon zest, heavy cream, and a pinch of salt.
- Place the bowl over a pot of simmering water (double boiler method), making sure the water doesn't touch the bottom of the bowl. Cook the mixture, whisking constantly, until it thickens and coats the back of a spoon, about 8-10 minutes.
- Remove the bowl from heat and whisk in the cubed butter until melted and smooth.

3. Assemble and Bake the Tart:

- Pour the lemon filling into the pre-baked tart crust, smoothing the top with a spatula.
- Return the tart to the oven and bake for 10-12 minutes, or until the filling is set and slightly jiggly in the center.

4. Chill and Serve:

- Remove the tart from the oven and let it cool completely on a wire rack.
- Once cooled, refrigerate the tart for at least 2 hours, or until chilled and set.
- Optionally, dust the tart with powdered sugar before serving.

5. Enjoy:

- Slice the Lemon Tart and serve chilled. It's wonderfully tangy and refreshing, perfect for any occasion.

Tips:

- **Make-Ahead:** You can prepare the tart crust and lemon filling ahead of time. Store the baked crust and cooled filling separately in the refrigerator, then assemble and bake the tart just before serving.
- **Zesting Lemons:** Use a fine grater or zester to zest the lemons, being careful to only grate the outer yellow peel and not the bitter white pith.
- **Variations:** For a twist, you can add a meringue topping (similar to a Lemon Meringue Pie) or garnish with fresh berries before serving.

Enjoy creating this delightful Tarte au Citron, a perfect balance of sweet and tart flavors with a buttery crust!

Chouquettes

Ingredients:

- 1/2 cup (120ml) water
- 1/2 cup (120ml) whole milk
- 1/2 cup (115g) unsalted butter, cut into cubes
- 1 tablespoon granulated sugar
- 1/4 teaspoon salt
- 1 cup (125g) all-purpose flour
- 4 large eggs
- Pearl sugar, for topping (available in baking supply stores or online)

Instructions:

1. Prepare the Choux Pastry Dough:

- Preheat your oven to 400°F (200°C). Line a baking sheet with parchment paper.
- In a medium saucepan, combine the water, milk, butter, sugar, and salt. Bring to a simmer over medium heat, stirring occasionally, until the butter is melted.
- Reduce the heat to low and add the flour all at once. Stir vigorously with a wooden spoon until the mixture forms a smooth dough and pulls away from the sides of the pan. Cook for another minute or two to dry out the dough slightly.
- Transfer the dough to a mixing bowl or the bowl of a stand mixer fitted with a paddle attachment. Let it cool for a few minutes.

2. Incorporate the Eggs:

- Add the eggs, one at a time, mixing well after each addition. The dough should be smooth and shiny. It will initially look like it's separating, but keep mixing until it comes together.
- Continue mixing until you have a smooth, glossy dough that falls from the spoon in a V-shape.

3. Pipe and Bake the Chouquettes:

- Transfer the choux pastry dough to a piping bag fitted with a plain round tip (about 1/2 inch or 1.5 cm wide).
- Pipe small mounds of dough onto the prepared baking sheet, leaving space between them for spreading. Each mound should be about 1 inch (2.5 cm) in diameter.
- Sprinkle pearl sugar generously over the piped dough mounds.

4. Bake:

- Place the baking sheet in the preheated oven and immediately lower the temperature to 375°F (190°C).
- Bake for 20-25 minutes, or until the chouquettes are puffed up, golden brown, and crisp. Avoid opening the oven door during baking to prevent them from deflating.

5. Cool and Serve:

- Remove the chouquettes from the oven and transfer them to a wire rack to cool completely.
- Serve the chouquettes fresh, as they are or with a dusting of powdered sugar. They are best enjoyed on the day they are made.

Tips:

- **Pearl Sugar:** If you can't find pearl sugar, you can use coarse sugar or even regular granulated sugar. Pearl sugar adds a nice crunch and sweetness to the chouquettes.
- **Storage:** Chouquettes are best enjoyed fresh on the day they are baked. If you have leftovers, store them in an airtight container at room temperature for up to a day, but they may lose their crispiness.
- **Variations:** For a twist, you can fill the chouquettes with flavored whipped cream, pastry cream, or chocolate ganache using a piping bag fitted with a small round tip. Simply insert the tip into the bottom of each chouquette and fill until slightly plump.

Enjoy baking these delightful Chouquettes and savoring their light, airy texture and sweet crunchiness!

Paris-Brest

Ingredients:

For the Choux Pastry:

- 1/2 cup (120ml) water
- 1/2 cup (120ml) whole milk
- 1/2 cup (115g) unsalted butter, cut into cubes
- 1 tablespoon granulated sugar
- 1/4 teaspoon salt
- 1 cup (125g) all-purpose flour
- 4 large eggs

For the Praline Cream:

- 1 cup (240ml) whole milk
- 4 large egg yolks
- 1/4 cup (50g) granulated sugar
- 2 tablespoons cornstarch
- 1 teaspoon vanilla extract
- 1/2 cup (120ml) heavy cream
- 1/2 cup (120g) praline paste (or hazelnut paste)

For Garnish:

- Sliced almonds
- Powdered sugar, for dusting

Instructions:

1. Make the Choux Pastry:

- Preheat your oven to 400°F (200°C). Line a baking sheet with parchment paper.
- In a medium saucepan, combine the water, milk, butter, sugar, and salt. Bring to a simmer over medium heat, stirring occasionally, until the butter is melted.
- Reduce the heat to low and add the flour all at once. Stir vigorously with a wooden spoon until the mixture forms a smooth dough and pulls away from the sides of the pan. Cook for another minute or two to dry out the dough slightly.
- Transfer the dough to a mixing bowl or the bowl of a stand mixer fitted with a paddle attachment. Let it cool for a few minutes.
- Add the eggs, one at a time, mixing well after each addition. The dough should be smooth and shiny. It will initially look like it's separating, but keep mixing until it comes together.

- Transfer the dough to a piping bag fitted with a large round tip (about 1/2 inch or 1.5 cm wide). Pipe a ring shape onto the prepared baking sheet, about 10 inches (25 cm) in diameter, with a smaller inner circle about 5 inches (12 cm) in diameter. Smooth the surface with a wet finger.
- Sprinkle sliced almonds over the piped dough.
- Bake at 400°F (200°C) for 15 minutes, then reduce the oven temperature to 350°F (180°C) and bake for another 25-30 minutes, or until the pastry is golden brown and crisp. Remove from the oven and let cool completely on a wire rack.

2. Make the Praline Cream:

- In a saucepan, heat the milk until steaming (do not boil).
- In a bowl, whisk together the egg yolks, sugar, and cornstarch until pale and creamy.
- Gradually whisk the hot milk into the egg mixture. Return the mixture to the saucepan and cook over medium heat, stirring constantly, until thickened.
- Remove from heat and stir in the vanilla extract. Transfer to a bowl, cover with plastic wrap (pressing the wrap onto the surface of the cream to prevent a skin from forming), and refrigerate until completely chilled.
- In a separate bowl, whip the heavy cream until stiff peaks form. Gently fold the whipped cream and praline paste into the chilled pastry cream until smooth and well combined.

3. Assemble the Paris-Brest:

- Once the choux pastry ring has cooled completely, carefully slice it horizontally using a serrated knife.
- Fill the bottom half of the pastry ring with the praline cream mixture.
- Place the top half of the pastry ring over the cream, gently pressing down.
- Dust the Paris-Brest with powdered sugar.

4. Serve:

- Slice and serve the Paris-Brest immediately. It's best enjoyed fresh on the day it's made.

Tips:

- **Praline Paste:** If you can't find praline paste, you can make your own by blending equal parts toasted hazelnuts or almonds with powdered sugar until smooth.
- **Garnish:** You can garnish the Paris-Brest with additional sliced almonds or powdered sugar for an elegant presentation.
- **Storage:** Paris-Brest is best enjoyed fresh. If you have leftovers, store them in the refrigerator, but note that the choux pastry may lose some of its crispness.

Enjoy making and savoring this decadent Paris-Brest, a beloved French pastry that combines crisp choux pastry with creamy praline filling!

Gougères

Ingredients:

- 1/2 cup (120ml) water
- 1/2 cup (120ml) whole milk
- 1/2 cup (115g) unsalted butter, cut into cubes
- 1/2 teaspoon salt
- 1 cup (125g) all-purpose flour
- 4 large eggs
- 1 cup (100g) grated Gruyère cheese (or another cheese of your choice)
- Freshly ground black pepper, to taste
- Pinch of nutmeg (optional)

Instructions:

1. Preheat Oven and Prepare Baking Sheets:

- Preheat your oven to 425°F (220°C). Line two baking sheets with parchment paper.

2. Make the Choux Pastry:

- In a medium saucepan, combine water, milk, butter, and salt. Bring to a simmer over medium heat, stirring occasionally, until the butter is melted.
- Reduce the heat to low, add the flour all at once, and stir vigorously with a wooden spoon until the mixture forms a smooth dough. Cook for another minute or two to dry out the dough slightly.
- Transfer the dough to a mixing bowl or the bowl of a stand mixer fitted with a paddle attachment. Let it cool for a few minutes.

3. Incorporate the Eggs:

- Add the eggs, one at a time, mixing well after each addition. The dough should be smooth and shiny. It will initially look like it's separating, but keep mixing until it comes together.
- Stir in the grated Gruyère cheese, black pepper, and nutmeg (if using), until well combined.

4. Form and Bake the Gougères:

- Using a spoon or a small cookie scoop, drop rounded tablespoonfuls of dough onto the prepared baking sheets, spacing them about 2 inches (5 cm) apart.
- Alternatively, you can pipe the dough into small mounds using a piping bag fitted with a plain round tip.

5. Bake:

- Bake the Gougères in the preheated oven for 15 minutes.
- After 15 minutes, reduce the oven temperature to 375°F (190°C) and continue baking for another 10-15 minutes, or until the Gougères are puffed up, golden brown, and crispy.

6. Serve:

- Remove from the oven and let the Gougères cool slightly on the baking sheets before transferring them to a wire rack to cool completely.
- Serve warm or at room temperature. They are best enjoyed fresh on the day they are made.

Tips:

- **Cheese Variations:** While Gruyère is traditional, you can experiment with other cheeses such as Emmental, Cheddar, or Parmesan. Just make sure to use a cheese that melts well and adds good flavor.
- **Seasoning:** Feel free to customize the seasoning with herbs like thyme or rosemary, or add a pinch of cayenne pepper for a bit of heat.
- **Storage:** Gougères are best enjoyed fresh, but you can store any leftovers in an airtight container at room temperature for up to 2 days. Reheat them in a 350°F (175°C) oven for a few minutes to regain their crispiness.

These Gougères make a delightful appetizer or snack, perfect for serving at parties or enjoying with a glass of wine. Enjoy baking and savoring these cheesy, savory puffs!

Bûche de Noël (Yule Log)

Ingredients:

For the Chocolate Genoise Cake:

- 4 large eggs
- 2/3 cup (130g) granulated sugar
- 1/2 cup (60g) all-purpose flour
- 1/4 cup (30g) unsweetened cocoa powder
- Pinch of salt
- 2 tablespoons unsalted butter, melted and cooled

For the Coffee Buttercream:

- 1 cup (225g) unsalted butter, softened
- 1 1/2 cups (180g) powdered sugar, sifted
- 2 tablespoons instant coffee granules dissolved in 1 tablespoon hot water
- 1 teaspoon vanilla extract

For the Chocolate Ganache Frosting:

- 8 ounces (225g) semi-sweet chocolate, finely chopped
- 1 cup (240ml) heavy cream

For Decoration:

- Cocoa powder, for dusting
- Meringue mushrooms (optional)
- Sprigs of rosemary or edible decorations (optional)

Instructions:

1. Make the Chocolate Genoise Cake:

- Preheat your oven to 350°F (175°C). Grease a 15x10-inch (38x25cm) jelly roll pan or rimmed baking sheet and line it with parchment paper.
- In a heatproof bowl, whisk together the eggs and granulated sugar. Place the bowl over a pot of simmering water (double boiler) and whisk constantly until the mixture reaches 110°F (45°C) or until it is warm to the touch.
- Remove from heat and continue whisking until the mixture is pale, thick, and tripled in volume, about 5-7 minutes.
- In a separate bowl, sift together the flour, cocoa powder, and salt.
- Gently fold the flour mixture into the egg mixture in three additions, using a spatula. Fold in the melted butter until just combined.

- Spread the batter evenly into the prepared pan and bake for 12-15 minutes, or until the cake springs back when lightly pressed.
- Immediately invert the cake onto a clean kitchen towel dusted with cocoa powder. Carefully peel off the parchment paper and roll up the cake from the short end with the towel inside. Let it cool completely on a wire rack.

2. Make the Coffee Buttercream:

- In a mixing bowl, beat the softened butter until creamy and smooth.
- Gradually add the powdered sugar, beating until light and fluffy.
- Add the dissolved instant coffee and vanilla extract. Beat until well combined and smooth. Set aside.

3. Assemble the Bûche de Noël:

- Carefully unroll the cooled cake and spread the coffee buttercream evenly over the inside surface of the cake, leaving a small border around the edges.
- Re-roll the cake without the towel, starting from the same short end. Place the seam side down on a serving platter or cake board.

4. Make the Chocolate Ganache Frosting:

- Place the chopped chocolate in a heatproof bowl.
- In a small saucepan, heat the heavy cream until it just begins to simmer. Pour the hot cream over the chopped chocolate and let it sit for 1-2 minutes.
- Gently stir the ganache with a spatula until smooth and shiny. Let it cool slightly until it thickens to a spreadable consistency.

5. Frost and Decorate the Bûche de Noël:

- Spread the chocolate ganache frosting over the rolled cake, using a spatula to create a bark-like texture.
- Drag a fork or a decorating comb gently through the ganache to create the look of tree bark.
- Decorate with cocoa powder dusted over the log, meringue mushrooms, and sprigs of rosemary or other edible decorations as desired.

6. Serve:

- Chill the Bûche de Noël in the refrigerator for at least 1 hour before serving to set the frosting.
- Slice and serve the Bûche de Noël chilled, enjoying its festive appearance and delicious flavors.

Tips:

- **Genoise Cake:** The genoise cake should be rolled while warm to prevent cracking. Rolling it with a towel helps maintain its shape.
- **Buttercream:** Adjust the intensity of coffee flavor by varying the amount of instant coffee used in the buttercream.
- **Ganache:** Make sure the ganache has cooled and thickened enough to spread easily but not slide off the cake.
- **Decoration:** Have fun with decorating your Bûche de Noël! Meringue mushrooms add a whimsical touch, but you can also use marzipan decorations, powdered sugar snow, or other edible decorations to enhance the festive look.

Enjoy making and sharing this traditional French holiday dessert, Bûche de Noël, with your loved ones!

Kouign-Amann

Ingredients:

For the Dough:

- 2 cups (250g) all-purpose flour, plus extra for dusting
- 1 teaspoon instant yeast
- 3/4 teaspoon salt
- 3/4 cup (180ml) lukewarm water
- 1 tablespoon unsalted butter, melted

For the Butter Block:

- 1 cup (225g) unsalted butter, cold
- 1/2 cup (100g) granulated sugar, for layering

For Assembly:

- Additional granulated sugar, for sprinkling
- Sea salt flakes (optional, for sprinkling)

Instructions:

1. Prepare the Dough:

- In a large bowl, combine the flour, instant yeast, and salt.
- Add the lukewarm water and melted butter to the dry ingredients. Mix until the dough comes together.
- Turn the dough out onto a lightly floured surface and knead for about 5-7 minutes, or until smooth and elastic. Shape the dough into a ball.
- Place the dough ball in a lightly oiled bowl, cover with plastic wrap, and let it rise in a warm place for about 1 hour, or until doubled in size.

2. Prepare the Butter Block:

- While the dough is rising, prepare the butter block. Place the cold unsalted butter between two sheets of parchment paper or plastic wrap. Using a rolling pin, pound and roll the butter into a rectangle about 1/2 inch (1.3cm) thick. Alternatively, you can use a stand mixer with a paddle attachment to soften and shape the butter.
- Transfer the butter block to the refrigerator to chill until firm but still pliable.

3. Laminate the Dough:

- On a lightly floured surface, roll out the risen dough into a large rectangle, about 12x18 inches (30x45cm).

- Place the chilled butter block in the center of the dough rectangle. Fold the dough over the butter block, sealing the edges tightly to encase the butter completely.
- Turn the dough 90 degrees and roll it out into a long rectangle, about 8x24 inches (20x60cm).
- Sprinkle half of the granulated sugar evenly over the rolled-out dough. Fold the dough into thirds like a business letter, starting with the bottom third up and then folding the top third down over it.
- Wrap the dough in plastic wrap and refrigerate for about 30 minutes to chill and relax the gluten.

4. Shape and Bake the Kouign-Amann:

- Preheat your oven to 400°F (200°C). Butter a muffin tin or line it with parchment paper.
- On a lightly floured surface, roll out the chilled dough into a large rectangle, about 10x16 inches (25x40cm) and 1/4 inch (6mm) thick.
- Sprinkle the remaining granulated sugar evenly over the rolled-out dough. Use a rolling pin to lightly press the sugar into the dough.
- Cut the dough into squares, about 4x4 inches (10x10cm) each.
- Working with one square at a time, fold each corner of the square towards the center to form a small package or pouch. Press the dough slightly to seal the corners together.
- Place each shaped Kouign-Amann into the prepared muffin tin, with the sealed corners facing up.
- Sprinkle each Kouign-Amann with a pinch of sea salt flakes (optional) and a little extra granulated sugar.

5. Bake and Serve:

- Bake the Kouign-Amann in the preheated oven for 30-35 minutes, or until they are deeply golden brown and caramelized.
- Remove the muffin tin from the oven and let the Kouign-Amann cool in the tin for 5 minutes before transferring them to a wire rack to cool completely.
- Serve the Kouign-Amann warm or at room temperature. They are best enjoyed fresh on the day they are made.

Tips:

- **Butter Quality:** Use high-quality unsalted butter for the best flavor and texture in your Kouign-Amann.
- **Sugar:** The layers of sugar create the caramelized, crispy exterior of the pastry. Don't skip or reduce the sugar in the recipe.
- **Storage:** Kouign-Amann are best enjoyed fresh. If you have leftovers, store them in an airtight container at room temperature for up to 2 days. Reheat briefly in the oven before serving to restore their crispiness.

Enjoy baking this indulgent and delicious Kouign-Amann pastry at home, savoring each flaky, buttery bite!

Pithiviers

Ingredients:

For the Almond Filling:

- 1 cup (100g) almond flour or finely ground almonds
- 1/2 cup (100g) granulated sugar
- 1/4 cup (60g) unsalted butter, softened
- 1 large egg
- 1 teaspoon almond extract
- Zest of 1 lemon (optional)

For the Puff Pastry:

- 1 sheet (about 14 oz or 400g) store-bought puff pastry, thawed if frozen
- 1 egg yolk, beaten (for egg wash)
- Powdered sugar, for dusting (optional)

Instructions:

1. Make the Almond Filling:

- In a mixing bowl, combine the almond flour (or ground almonds), granulated sugar, softened butter, egg, almond extract, and lemon zest (if using). Mix until smooth and well combined. Set aside.

2. Prepare the Puff Pastry:

- Roll out the puff pastry sheet on a lightly floured surface into a large circle, about 12 inches (30 cm) in diameter, and 1/8 inch (3 mm) thick.
- Using a 9-inch (23 cm) round cake pan or plate as a guide, cut out two circles from the puff pastry. These will be the top and bottom layers of your Pithiviers.

3. Assemble the Pithiviers:

- Place one of the puff pastry circles on a parchment-lined baking sheet.
- Spoon the almond filling onto the center of the puff pastry circle, leaving a border of about 1 inch (2.5 cm) around the edge.
- Brush the exposed border of the puff pastry with beaten egg yolk.
- Carefully place the second puff pastry circle on top of the almond filling.
- Press down the edges to seal, and crimp them with a fork or your fingers to create a decorative edge. Trim any excess pastry if necessary.

4. Decorate the Pithiviers (optional):

- Using a sharp knife, lightly score a decorative pattern (such as a lattice or concentric circles) on the top layer of puff pastry. Be careful not to cut all the way through.

5. Bake the Pithiviers:

- Preheat your oven to 400°F (200°C).
- Brush the top of the Pithiviers with more beaten egg yolk for a shiny finish.
- Bake in the preheated oven for 25-30 minutes, or until the Pithiviers is puffed and golden brown.

6. Serve:

- Remove from the oven and let the Pithiviers cool slightly on the baking sheet.
- Optionally, dust with powdered sugar before serving.

7. Enjoy:

- Slice the Pithiviers and serve warm or at room temperature. It pairs wonderfully with a cup of coffee or tea.

Tips:

- **Almond Filling Variations:** You can add chopped almonds or a dash of rum or brandy to the almond filling for extra flavor.
- **Puff Pastry:** If you prefer to make your own puff pastry, you can find recipes online or use store-bought for convenience.
- **Decoration:** Get creative with the decorative pattern on top of your Pithiviers. It adds to the presentation and can be tailored to suit your preference.

Pithiviers is a delightful pastry that showcases the richness of almond filling and the flakiness of puff pastry. Enjoy baking and sharing this classic French treat with family and friends!

Tarte aux Fraises (Strawberry Tart)

Ingredients:

For the Tart Shell:

- 1 1/4 cups (160g) all-purpose flour
- 1/4 cup (30g) powdered sugar
- 1/4 teaspoon salt
- 1/2 cup (115g) unsalted butter, cold and cut into cubes
- 1 large egg yolk
- 1-2 tablespoons ice water

For the Pastry Cream:

- 1 cup (240ml) whole milk
- 1/2 vanilla bean, split lengthwise (or 1 teaspoon vanilla extract)
- 3 large egg yolks
- 1/4 cup (50g) granulated sugar
- 2 tablespoons cornstarch
- 2 tablespoons unsalted butter
- Fresh strawberries, hulled and sliced

For Glaze (optional):

- 1/4 cup apricot jam
- 1 tablespoon water

Instructions:

1. Make the Tart Shell:

- In a food processor, combine the flour, powdered sugar, and salt. Pulse to mix.
- Add the cold butter cubes and pulse until the mixture resembles coarse crumbs.
- Add the egg yolk and 1 tablespoon of ice water. Pulse again until the dough starts to come together. Add more ice water, 1 teaspoon at a time, if needed.
- Turn out the dough onto a lightly floured surface and gather into a ball. Flatten into a disc, wrap in plastic wrap, and refrigerate for at least 1 hour.
- Preheat your oven to 375°F (190°C). Roll out the chilled dough on a lightly floured surface to fit into a 9-inch (23cm) tart pan with a removable bottom. Press the dough into the pan, trim the excess, and prick the bottom with a fork.
- Line the tart shell with parchment paper and fill with pie weights or dried beans. Bake for 15 minutes. Remove the weights and parchment paper, then bake for another 10-12 minutes, or until the crust is golden brown. Let cool completely.

2. Make the Pastry Cream:

- In a saucepan, heat the milk and vanilla bean (scraped seeds and pod) over medium heat until just simmering. Remove from heat and let steep for 10-15 minutes. If using vanilla extract, add it after steeping.
- In a bowl, whisk together the egg yolks, sugar, and cornstarch until pale and thick.
- Remove the vanilla bean pod from the milk mixture. Gradually whisk the warm milk into the egg mixture.
- Pour the mixture back into the saucepan and cook over medium heat, whisking constantly, until it thickens and comes to a boil. Boil for 1-2 minutes, then remove from heat.
- Stir in the butter until melted and smooth. Transfer the pastry cream to a bowl, cover with plastic wrap (pressing directly onto the surface to prevent a skin from forming), and chill in the refrigerator until cold.

3. Assemble the Tart:

- Spread the chilled pastry cream evenly into the cooled tart shell.
- Arrange the sliced strawberries on top of the pastry cream in a decorative pattern.

4. Optional Glaze:

- In a small saucepan, heat the apricot jam and water until melted and smooth. Strain through a fine mesh sieve to remove any fruit pieces.
- Brush the warm glaze over the strawberries to give them a shiny finish. Allow the glaze to set for a few minutes.

5. Serve:

- Slice and serve the Tarte aux Fraises chilled. Enjoy the buttery crust, creamy pastry cream, and fresh strawberries!

Tips:

- **Strawberry Selection:** Choose ripe, fresh strawberries that are firm and fragrant for the best flavor and appearance.
- **Make-Ahead:** You can prepare the tart shell and pastry cream ahead of time. Assemble the tart with strawberries shortly before serving to keep the crust crisp.
- **Variations:** Feel free to experiment with other fruits or berries for different variations of this tart. Raspberries, blueberries, or a mix of berries can also be delicious.

This Tarte aux Fraises is sure to impress with its elegant presentation and delicious flavors. Perfect for a special occasion or as a delightful dessert to celebrate the sweetness of fresh strawberries!

Palmiers

Ingredients:

- 1 sheet of puff pastry (store-bought or homemade), thawed if frozen
- 1 cup (200g) granulated sugar
- Pinch of salt
- Optional: 1/2 teaspoon ground cinnamon or other spices (optional)

Instructions:

1. Prepare the Puff Pastry:

- If using store-bought puff pastry, follow the package instructions to thaw it. If making homemade puff pastry, ensure it is rolled out into a large rectangle about 1/4 inch (6mm) thick.

2. Prepare the Sugar Mixture:

- In a shallow bowl or plate, mix together the granulated sugar, salt, and ground cinnamon (if using). This will be used to coat the palmiers.

3. Shape the Palmiers:

- Sprinkle a clean work surface with a generous amount of the sugar mixture.
- Place the puff pastry sheet on top of the sugar mixture and roll it out slightly to press the sugar into the pastry.
- Fold the two opposite long sides of the puff pastry towards the center so they meet in the middle, creating a long rectangular strip.
- Fold the strip in half along the center line to create a double-layered log. Press gently to seal the layers together.
- Using a sharp knife, slice the log crosswise into pieces about 1/2 inch (1.25 cm) thick.

4. Bake the Palmiers:

- Preheat your oven to 400°F (200°C). Line a baking sheet with parchment paper.
- Place the sliced palmiers on the prepared baking sheet, cut-side down, leaving space between them to allow for spreading.
- Sprinkle additional sugar mixture over the tops of the palmiers.
- Bake in the preheated oven for 15-20 minutes, or until the palmiers are golden brown and caramelized. Keep an eye on them towards the end of baking to prevent burning.

5. Cool and Serve:

- Remove the baked palmiers from the oven and let them cool on the baking sheet for a few minutes.

- Transfer the palmiers to a wire rack to cool completely. They will continue to crisp up as they cool.

6. Enjoy:

- Serve the palmiers at room temperature. They are best enjoyed fresh on the day they are made.

Tips:

- **Puff Pastry Quality:** Use high-quality puff pastry for the best results. Homemade puff pastry can also be used if you prefer.
- **Sugar Coating:** Ensure the sugar mixture is well distributed and pressed into the puff pastry to achieve caramelization during baking.
- **Variations:** Experiment with different flavors by adding spices like cinnamon, nutmeg, or cardamom to the sugar mixture. You can also add a thin layer of Nutella or jam before folding for a different twist.
- **Storage:** Palmiers are best enjoyed fresh and crispy. Store any leftovers in an airtight container at room temperature for up to 2 days. Reheat briefly in the oven to regain crispiness if needed.

Palmiers are a delightful treat with their crisp texture and sweet caramelized flavor. They make a perfect accompaniment to coffee or tea, or a lovely addition to a dessert platter. Enjoy making and savoring these French pastries at home!

Canelés de Bordeaux

Ingredients:

- 2 cups (480ml) whole milk
- 2 tablespoons (30g) unsalted butter
- 1 vanilla bean, split lengthwise (or 1 teaspoon vanilla extract)
- 1 1/4 cups (250g) granulated sugar
- 1 cup (125g) all-purpose flour
- Pinch of salt
- 3 large eggs
- 1 large egg yolk
- 1/4 cup (60ml) dark rum (or rum extract)
- Butter or nonstick cooking spray, for greasing molds

Instructions:

1. Prepare the Batter:

- In a saucepan, combine the milk, butter, and vanilla bean (scraped seeds and pod). Heat over medium heat until the mixture comes to a simmer. Remove from heat and let cool to room temperature. If using vanilla extract, add it after the mixture has cooled.
- In a mixing bowl, whisk together the sugar, flour, and salt.
- Gradually whisk the eggs and egg yolk into the dry ingredients until smooth.
- Slowly pour in the cooled milk mixture, whisking constantly, until well combined and smooth.
- Stir in the rum (or rum extract). Cover the batter with plastic wrap, pressing it directly onto the surface to prevent a skin from forming. Refrigerate for at least 12 hours, preferably 24-48 hours.

2. Prepare the Molds:

- Butter or spray the canelé molds generously with butter or nonstick cooking spray. Place the molds on a baking sheet for stability.

3. Fill and Bake the Canelés:

- Preheat your oven to 450°F (230°C).
- Remove the batter from the refrigerator and stir gently to reincorporate any settled ingredients.
- Fill each canelé mold almost to the top with the chilled batter.
- Bake the canelés in the preheated oven for 10 minutes.
- Reduce the oven temperature to 375°F (190°C) and continue baking for another 50-60 minutes, or until the canelés are dark brown and caramelized on the outside.

4. Cool and Unmold:

- Remove the canelés from the oven and let them cool in the molds for 10 minutes.
- Carefully unmold the canelés while they are still warm. Use a silicone spatula or gently tap the molds to release them.
- Transfer the canelés to a wire rack to cool completely.

5. Serve:

- Canelés de Bordeaux are best enjoyed slightly warm or at room temperature. They can be stored in an airtight container at room temperature for up to 2 days, but they are at their best on the day they are baked.

Tips:

- **Special Molds:** Canelés are traditionally baked in copper molds lined with beeswax. If using silicone molds, make sure they are of good quality and well-greased to ensure easy release.
- **Rum Flavor:** The rum adds a distinctive flavor to canelés. If you prefer a non-alcoholic version, you can use rum extract or omit it altogether, though the flavor will be slightly different.
- **Caramelization:** Achieving a deep caramelized crust is key to authentic canelés. Ensure your oven is hot enough initially and then reduced to allow the canelés to bake slowly and develop their characteristic color.

Canelés de Bordeaux are a wonderful treat with their contrasting textures and rich flavors. They make an elegant dessert or a delightful addition to a brunch or tea time. Enjoy baking these French delicacies and savoring their unique charm!

Pain Perdu (French Toast)

Ingredients:

- 4 slices of bread (day-old bread works best)
- 2 large eggs
- 1/2 cup (120ml) milk
- 1 tablespoon granulated sugar (optional, adjust to taste)
- 1/2 teaspoon vanilla extract
- Butter or neutral oil, for frying
- Toppings of your choice: maple syrup, powdered sugar, fresh berries, whipped cream, etc.

Instructions:

1. Prepare the Egg Mixture:

- In a shallow bowl or pie dish, whisk together the eggs, milk, sugar (if using), and vanilla extract until well combined. You can adjust the sweetness to your preference.

2. Soak the Bread:

- Heat a large skillet or frying pan over medium heat and add a knob of butter or a drizzle of neutral oil.
- Dip each slice of bread into the egg mixture, turning to coat both sides evenly. Allow the bread to soak for about 30 seconds on each side, ensuring it absorbs the mixture without becoming too soggy.

3. Fry the French Toast:

- Place the soaked bread slices in the preheated skillet. Cook for 2-3 minutes on each side, or until golden brown and cooked through.
- If needed, add more butter or oil to the skillet between batches to prevent sticking and ensure even cooking.

4. Serve:

- Remove the French toast slices from the skillet and transfer to serving plates.
- Serve immediately with your choice of toppings, such as maple syrup, powdered sugar, fresh berries, or whipped cream.

Tips:

- **Bread Selection:** Use thick slices of bread, preferably day-old bread or slightly stale bread, as it absorbs the egg mixture better without falling apart.

- **Flavor Variations:** Add a pinch of cinnamon or nutmeg to the egg mixture for extra flavor. You can also use almond extract or orange zest for a different twist.
- **Toppings:** Get creative with toppings! Besides traditional maple syrup and powdered sugar, try caramelized bananas, sliced almonds, or a dollop of yogurt.
- **Make-Ahead:** You can prepare the egg mixture in advance and store it in the refrigerator. Just give it a quick whisk before using.

Pain Perdu, or French Toast, is a comforting and versatile breakfast option that can be enjoyed by the whole family. It's perfect for lazy weekend mornings or special brunch occasions. Enjoy making and serving this classic French dish!

Tarte Normande

Ingredients:

For the Pastry:

- 1 1/4 cups (160g) all-purpose flour
- 1/4 cup (50g) granulated sugar
- Pinch of salt
- 1/2 cup (115g) unsalted butter, cold and cut into cubes
- 1 large egg yolk
- 1-2 tablespoons ice water

For the Filling:

- 3-4 large apples (such as Granny Smith or Braeburn), peeled, cored, and thinly sliced
- 2 tablespoons unsalted butter, melted
- 1/4 cup (50g) granulated sugar
- 2 large eggs
- 1/2 cup (120ml) heavy cream (or crème fraîche)
- 1/4 cup (60ml) milk
- 1 teaspoon vanilla extract
- 1/4 teaspoon ground cinnamon (optional)
- Confectioners' sugar, for dusting

Instructions:

1. Prepare the Pastry:

- In a food processor, combine the flour, sugar, and salt. Pulse to mix.
- Add the cold butter cubes and pulse until the mixture resembles coarse crumbs.
- Add the egg yolk and 1 tablespoon of ice water. Pulse again until the dough starts to come together. Add more ice water, 1 teaspoon at a time, if needed.
- Turn out the dough onto a lightly floured surface and gather into a ball. Flatten into a disc, wrap in plastic wrap, and refrigerate for at least 1 hour.

2. Prepare the Filling:

- Preheat your oven to 375°F (190°C).
- In a large bowl, toss the sliced apples with melted butter and granulated sugar until evenly coated.
- In another bowl, whisk together the eggs, heavy cream (or crème fraîche), milk, vanilla extract, and ground cinnamon (if using) until well combined.

3. Assemble the Tarte Normande:

- On a lightly floured surface, roll out the chilled pastry dough into a circle about 12 inches (30cm) in diameter. Carefully transfer the dough to a 9-inch (23cm) tart pan with a removable bottom. Press the dough into the pan and trim any excess.
- Arrange the sliced apples evenly over the bottom of the pastry shell.
- Pour the custard mixture over the apples, making sure it fills the tart shell evenly.

4. Bake the Tarte Normande:

- Place the tart pan on a baking sheet (to catch any drips) and bake in the preheated oven for 35-40 minutes, or until the custard is set and the pastry is golden brown.
- Remove the tart from the oven and let it cool on a wire rack for at least 15 minutes.

5. Serve:

- Dust the cooled Tarte Normande with confectioners' sugar before serving.
- Slice and serve the tart warm or at room temperature. It pairs beautifully with a dollop of whipped cream or a scoop of vanilla ice cream.

Tips:

- **Apple Selection:** Choose firm apples that hold their shape when baked, such as Granny Smith or Braeburn. You can mix different varieties for a more complex flavor.
- **Custard Consistency:** Ensure the custard is fully set before removing the tart from the oven. It should jiggle slightly in the center but not be liquidy.
- **Make-Ahead:** You can prepare the pastry dough and custard filling in advance. Store the dough wrapped in plastic wrap in the refrigerator and the custard covered in the fridge. Assemble and bake the tart just before serving for the best results.

Tarte Normande is a wonderful dessert that showcases the natural sweetness of apples complemented by the rich custard filling and buttery pastry. Enjoy making this classic French tart and sharing it with friends and family!

Tarte aux Pommes (Apple Tart)

Ingredients:

For the Pastry:

- 1 1/4 cups (160g) all-purpose flour
- 1/4 cup (50g) granulated sugar
- Pinch of salt
- 1/2 cup (115g) unsalted butter, cold and cut into cubes
- 1 large egg yolk
- 1-2 tablespoons ice water

For the Apple Filling:

- 4-5 medium apples (such as Granny Smith, Honeycrisp, or Gala)
- 2 tablespoons unsalted butter, melted
- 2 tablespoons apricot preserves or apple jelly (for glaze)
- Juice of 1/2 lemon
- 1/4 cup (50g) granulated sugar
- 1/2 teaspoon ground cinnamon (optional)

For Assembly:

- Confectioners' sugar, for dusting

Instructions:

1. Prepare the Pastry:

- In a food processor, combine the flour, sugar, and salt. Pulse to mix.
- Add the cold butter cubes and pulse until the mixture resembles coarse crumbs.
- Add the egg yolk and 1 tablespoon of ice water. Pulse again until the dough starts to come together. Add more ice water, 1 teaspoon at a time, if needed.
- Turn out the dough onto a lightly floured surface and gather into a ball. Flatten into a disc, wrap in plastic wrap, and refrigerate for at least 1 hour.

2. Prepare the Apples:

- Peel, core, and thinly slice the apples. Toss the apple slices with lemon juice to prevent browning.

3. Roll out the Pastry:

- Preheat your oven to 375°F (190°C).

- On a lightly floured surface, roll out the chilled pastry dough into a circle about 12 inches (30cm) in diameter. Carefully transfer the dough to a 9-inch (23cm) tart pan with a removable bottom. Press the dough into the pan and trim any excess.

4. Arrange the Apple Filling:

- Starting from the outer edge of the tart shell, arrange the apple slices in overlapping concentric circles, working your way towards the center.
- Brush the melted butter over the arranged apples. Sprinkle the granulated sugar and ground cinnamon (if using) evenly over the apples.

5. Bake the Tart:

- Place the tart pan on a baking sheet (to catch any drips) and bake in the preheated oven for 35-40 minutes, or until the pastry is golden brown and the apples are tender.

6. Glaze the Tart:

- In a small saucepan, heat the apricot preserves or apple jelly over low heat until melted and smooth.
- Remove the tart from the oven and brush the melted preserves/jelly over the warm apples to glaze them.

7. Serve:

- Let the Tarte aux Pommes cool slightly in the tart pan before carefully removing the outer ring.
- Dust the tart with confectioners' sugar just before serving.

8. Enjoy:

- Serve the Tarte aux Pommes warm or at room temperature. It can be enjoyed on its own or with a scoop of vanilla ice cream or a dollop of whipped cream.

Tips:

- **Apple Selection:** Choose firm apples that hold their shape well when baked. Varieties like Granny Smith, Honeycrisp, or Gala are great options for baking.
- **Pastry Crust:** Ensure the pastry crust is well-chilled before rolling it out to prevent shrinking during baking.
- **Glaze Variation:** If apricot preserves or apple jelly are not available, you can brush the warm apples with a simple syrup or honey for a glossy finish.
- **Make-Ahead:** You can prepare the pastry dough and slice the apples in advance. Assemble and bake the tart just before serving for the freshest results.

Tarte aux Pommes is a delightful dessert that beautifully combines the crisp texture of apples with the buttery richness of pastry. It's perfect for showcasing seasonal apples and is sure to impress your guests with its simple yet elegant presentation. Enjoy baking and savoring this classic French treat!

Crème Brûlée

Ingredients:

- 1 quart (4 cups or 960ml) heavy cream
- 1 vanilla bean, split lengthwise (or 1 teaspoon vanilla extract)
- 6 large egg yolks
- 3/4 cup (150g) granulated sugar, divided
- Pinch of salt
- Extra granulated sugar, for caramelizing

Instructions:

1. Preheat the Oven:

- Preheat your oven to 325°F (160°C). Place a large roasting pan or baking dish in the oven and fill it with enough hot water to come halfway up the sides of the ramekins later (this will be used for baking the custards in a water bath).

2. Prepare the Custard:

- In a saucepan, combine the heavy cream and the scraped seeds from the vanilla bean (or vanilla extract). Heat over medium heat until just simmering. Remove from heat and let it steep for about 15 minutes to infuse the cream with vanilla flavor. If using vanilla extract, add it after steeping.
- In a mixing bowl, whisk together the egg yolks, 1/2 cup (100g) of granulated sugar, and a pinch of salt until smooth and pale yellow.
- Gradually pour the warm cream mixture into the egg yolk mixture, whisking constantly, to temper the eggs and prevent scrambling.

3. Strain the Mixture:

- Strain the custard mixture through a fine-mesh sieve into a large measuring cup or pitcher, discarding the vanilla bean pod (if used) and any solids.

4. Bake the Custards:

- Arrange six 6-ounce (180ml) ramekins in the preheated water-filled roasting pan or baking dish. Carefully pour the custard mixture into the ramekins, dividing it evenly.
- Place the roasting pan in the oven and bake for 30-35 minutes, or until the edges are set but the centers still jiggle slightly when gently shaken.

5. Chill the Custards:

- Carefully remove the ramekins from the water bath and let them cool to room temperature on a wire rack. Once cooled, cover each ramekin with plastic wrap and refrigerate for at least 4 hours, preferably overnight, to chill and set completely.

6. Caramelize the Sugar:

- Just before serving, evenly sprinkle about 1 tablespoon of granulated sugar over the surface of each custard.
- Using a kitchen torch, carefully and evenly caramelize the sugar until it forms a golden-brown crust. Alternatively, you can place the ramekins under a preheated broiler for 1-2 minutes until the sugar melts and caramelizes (watch closely to prevent burning).

7. Serve:

- Let the Crème Brûlée sit for a few minutes to allow the caramelized sugar to harden.
- Serve immediately, garnished with berries or mint leaves if desired.

Tips:

- **Vanilla Bean Substitution:** If you don't have a vanilla bean, you can use 1 teaspoon of vanilla extract instead. Add it after steeping the cream.
- **Water Bath:** Baking the custards in a water bath ensures gentle, even cooking and helps prevent them from cracking.
- **Make-Ahead:** You can prepare the custard a day or two in advance and caramelize the sugar just before serving for the best texture.

Crème Brûlée is a decadent dessert that balances the smooth, creamy custard with the crisp caramelized sugar topping. It's a favorite in French cuisine for its luxurious texture and rich flavor. Enjoy making this classic dessert and impress your guests with its irresistible taste!

Mousse au Chocolat

Ingredients:

- 7 ounces (200g) dark chocolate (around 60-70% cocoa), chopped
- 4 large eggs, separated
- 1/4 cup (50g) granulated sugar
- Pinch of salt
- 1 teaspoon vanilla extract
- Optional: Whipped cream and chocolate shavings for garnish

Instructions:

1. Melt the Chocolate:

- Place the chopped dark chocolate in a heatproof bowl. Either microwave in 30-second intervals, stirring between each interval, or melt over a double boiler until smooth and melted. Set aside to cool slightly.

2. Prepare the Egg Yolks:

- In a mixing bowl, whisk the egg yolks with 2 tablespoons of sugar until pale and thickened.
- Whisk in the vanilla extract.
- Gradually whisk in the melted chocolate until well combined and smooth. Set aside.

3. Whip the Egg Whites:

- In a separate clean mixing bowl, using an electric mixer or whisk, beat the egg whites with a pinch of salt until soft peaks form.
- Gradually add the remaining 2 tablespoons of sugar while continuing to beat until stiff peaks form and the whites are glossy.

4. Combine and Fold:

- Fold about one-third of the beaten egg whites into the chocolate mixture using a spatula to lighten it.
- Gently fold in the remaining egg whites until no streaks remain, taking care not to deflate the mixture.

5. Chill:

- Spoon the chocolate mousse into serving glasses or bowls.
- Cover and refrigerate for at least 2 hours, or until set and chilled.

6. Serve:

- Before serving, optionally garnish with a dollop of whipped cream and chocolate shavings.
- Enjoy the Chocolate Mousse chilled and indulge in its creamy, decadent texture!

Tips:

- **Chocolate Selection:** Use good quality dark chocolate for the best flavor. Aim for chocolate with 60-70% cocoa content.
- **Egg Safety:** If you have concerns about consuming raw eggs, use pasteurized eggs or eggs that have been treated to reduce the risk of salmonella.
- **Folding Technique:** When folding in the egg whites, use a gentle motion to maintain the mousse's light and airy texture.
- **Make-Ahead:** You can prepare the chocolate mousse ahead of time and store it in the refrigerator until ready to serve. It can be chilled for several hours or overnight.

Chocolate Mousse is a classic French dessert that never fails to impress with its smooth and decadent flavor. Enjoy making this delightful dessert for special occasions or as a treat for yourself and loved ones!

Pralines

Ingredients:

- 1 cup (200g) granulated sugar
- 1 cup (220g) packed light brown sugar
- 1/2 cup (120ml) heavy cream
- 4 tablespoons (56g) unsalted butter
- 1/4 teaspoon salt
- 2 cups (240g) pecan halves
- 1 teaspoon vanilla extract

Instructions:

1. Prepare the Ingredients:

- Line a baking sheet with parchment paper or a silicone baking mat. Set aside.
- Measure out all your ingredients beforehand, as the cooking process for pralines moves quickly.

2. Cook the Praline Mixture:

- In a heavy-bottomed saucepan, combine the granulated sugar, brown sugar, heavy cream, butter, and salt over medium heat. Stir constantly until the butter melts and the sugar dissolves.
- Attach a candy thermometer to the side of the pan. Cook the mixture, stirring occasionally, until it reaches 240°F (115°C) on the thermometer (soft ball stage).

3. Add the Pecans:

- Once the mixture reaches 240°F (115°C), remove the pan from the heat.
- Stir in the pecan halves and vanilla extract until well coated with the caramel mixture.

4. Form the Pralines:

- Quickly drop spoonfuls of the hot praline mixture onto the prepared baking sheet. Work fast before the mixture starts to set.

5. Let the Pralines Cool:

- Let the pralines cool and harden at room temperature for about 30 minutes to 1 hour.

6. Enjoy:

- Once completely cooled and set, peel the pralines off the parchment paper and enjoy! Store any leftover pralines in an airtight container at room temperature for up to 1 week.

Tips:

- **Temperature Control:** Use a candy thermometer to ensure the caramel reaches the correct temperature (240°F or 115°C) for the best texture. This ensures the pralines set properly without being too soft or too hard.
- **Stirring Technique:** Stir the mixture gently and consistently to prevent the sugar from crystallizing and to evenly distribute the heat.
- **Variations:** You can customize pralines by using different nuts such as almonds or hazelnuts, or adding a pinch of cinnamon or a splash of bourbon for extra flavor.

Pralines are a delightful sweet treat that combines the crunch of nuts with the rich sweetness of caramelized sugar. Enjoy making these Southern classics at home and sharing them with friends and family!

Galette Bretonne

Ingredients:

For the Galette Batter:

- 1 cup (120g) buckwheat flour
- 1/2 teaspoon salt
- 2 large eggs
- 1 1/4 cups (300ml) water
- 1 tablespoon unsalted butter, melted (plus extra for cooking)

For the Filling (Example filling):

- 4 slices of ham (jambon)
- 1 cup (100g) grated Emmental or Gruyère cheese
- 4 large eggs
- Salt and pepper, to taste
- Chopped fresh herbs (such as parsley or chives), for garnish (optional)

Instructions:

1. Make the Galette Batter:

- In a mixing bowl, whisk together the buckwheat flour and salt.
- In a separate bowl, whisk the eggs and water until well combined.
- Gradually pour the egg mixture into the buckwheat flour mixture, whisking constantly to avoid lumps.
- Whisk in the melted butter until smooth. Cover the batter and let it rest at room temperature for at least 30 minutes (or up to 2 hours) to allow the flavors to develop.

2. Cook the Galettes:

- Heat a non-stick or cast iron skillet over medium heat. Brush the skillet lightly with melted butter.
- Pour about 1/4 cup of the galette batter into the skillet, swirling to evenly coat the bottom. Cook for 2-3 minutes, or until the edges start to lift and the bottom is golden brown.
- Flip the galette and cook for another 1-2 minutes on the other side. Remove from the skillet and keep warm. Repeat with the remaining batter, stacking the cooked galettes on a plate with parchment paper in between to prevent sticking.

3. Prepare the Filling:

- Preheat the oven to 350°F (175°C).

- Lay each galette flat on a baking sheet. Place a slice of ham on one half of each galette, then sprinkle with grated cheese.
- Crack an egg on top of the cheese. Season with salt and pepper.

4. Bake the Galettes:

- Fold the other half of the galette over the filling, creating a half-moon shape. Bake in the preheated oven for about 8-10 minutes, or until the egg is cooked to your liking and the cheese is melted.

5. Serve:

- Remove from the oven and garnish with chopped fresh herbs if desired. Serve hot, either as is or with a side salad.

Tips:

- **Buckwheat Flour:** Authentic Galette Bretonne uses buckwheat flour, which gives it a distinctive flavor and texture. You can find buckwheat flour in most grocery stores or online.
- **Filling Variations:** Feel free to customize the filling with ingredients like sautéed mushrooms, spinach, bacon, or different types of cheese. Be creative with your combinations!
- **Cooking Technique:** Cooking galettes requires a bit of practice to get the flipping right. Start with a smaller amount of batter and tilt the pan to spread it evenly.

Galette Bretonne is a comforting and satisfying dish that can be enjoyed for breakfast, lunch, or dinner. It's a versatile recipe that allows you to experiment with various fillings and flavors, making it a favorite in French cuisine. Bon appétit!

Tarte à la Rhubarbe (Rhubarb Tart)

Ingredients:

For the Pastry Dough:

- 1 1/4 cups (160g) all-purpose flour
- 1/4 cup (50g) granulated sugar
- Pinch of salt
- 1/2 cup (115g) unsalted butter, cold and cut into cubes
- 1 large egg yolk
- 1-2 tablespoons ice water

For the Rhubarb Filling:

- 4 cups (about 500g) rhubarb stalks, trimmed and cut into 1-inch pieces
- 1/2 cup (100g) granulated sugar (adjust to taste depending on the tartness of the rhubarb)
- 1 tablespoon cornstarch
- Zest and juice of 1 orange (optional)
- 1 teaspoon vanilla extract

For Assembly:

- Egg wash (1 egg beaten with 1 tablespoon water)
- Additional granulated sugar, for sprinkling

Instructions:

1. Prepare the Pastry Dough:

- In a food processor, combine the flour, sugar, and salt. Pulse to mix.
- Add the cold butter cubes and pulse until the mixture resembles coarse crumbs.
- Add the egg yolk and 1 tablespoon of ice water. Pulse again until the dough starts to come together. Add more ice water, 1 teaspoon at a time, if needed.
- Turn out the dough onto a lightly floured surface and gather into a ball. Flatten into a disc, wrap in plastic wrap, and refrigerate for at least 1 hour.

2. Prepare the Rhubarb Filling:

- In a large bowl, combine the rhubarb pieces, sugar, cornstarch, orange zest (if using), orange juice (if using), and vanilla extract. Toss gently to coat the rhubarb evenly. Let the mixture sit for about 15-20 minutes to allow the rhubarb to release some juices.

3. Roll out the Pastry and Assemble the Tart:

- Preheat your oven to 375°F (190°C). Line a baking sheet with parchment paper.
- On a lightly floured surface, roll out the chilled pastry dough into a circle about 12 inches (30cm) in diameter. Carefully transfer the dough to a 9-inch (23cm) tart pan with a removable bottom. Press the dough into the pan and trim any excess.
- Arrange the prepared rhubarb filling evenly over the pastry dough in the tart pan.

4. Bake the Tart:

- Brush the edges of the pastry with the egg wash and sprinkle lightly with granulated sugar.
- Place the tart pan on the lined baking sheet (to catch any drips) and bake in the preheated oven for 40-45 minutes, or until the pastry is golden brown and the rhubarb is tender.

5. Serve:

- Remove the tart from the oven and let it cool slightly on a wire rack before removing from the tart pan.
- Serve the Tarte à la Rhubarbe warm or at room temperature. Optionally, garnish with a dusting of powdered sugar or a dollop of whipped cream.

Tips:

- **Rhubarb Selection:** Choose firm, bright red or pink rhubarb stalks for the best color and flavor. If the rhubarb is very tart, you may want to increase the amount of sugar slightly.
- **Pastry Crust:** Ensure the pastry crust is well-chilled before rolling it out to prevent shrinking during baking.
- **Make-Ahead:** You can prepare the pastry dough and rhubarb filling in advance. Store the dough wrapped in plastic wrap in the refrigerator and the filling covered in the fridge. Assemble and bake the tart just before serving for the freshest results.

Tarte à la Rhubarbe is a wonderful way to enjoy the unique flavor of rhubarb in a beautifully presented dessert. It's perfect for spring and summer when rhubarb is in season. Enjoy baking and savoring this classic French tart!

Beignets

Ingredients:

- 1 cup (240ml) warm water (about 110°F or 45°C)
- 2 1/4 teaspoons (1 packet) active dry yeast
- 1/4 cup (50g) granulated sugar
- 1 teaspoon salt
- 2 large eggs
- 1/2 cup (120ml) evaporated milk or whole milk
- 4 cups (500g) all-purpose flour, plus more for dusting
- 1/4 cup (56g) unsalted butter, softened
- Vegetable oil, for frying
- Powdered sugar, for dusting

Instructions:

1. Activate the Yeast:

- In a small bowl, combine the warm water, yeast, and a pinch of sugar. Let it sit for about 5-10 minutes until frothy and bubbly.

2. Mix the Dough:

- In a large mixing bowl or the bowl of a stand mixer fitted with a dough hook, combine the yeast mixture with the sugar, salt, eggs, and evaporated milk (or whole milk).
- Gradually add the flour, mixing until a smooth dough forms. Add the softened butter and continue to knead until the dough is elastic and pulls away from the sides of the bowl, about 5-7 minutes.

3. Let the Dough Rise:

- Cover the bowl with plastic wrap or a clean kitchen towel and let the dough rise in a warm place until doubled in size, about 1-2 hours.

4. Roll and Cut the Beignets:

- Punch down the risen dough and turn it out onto a lightly floured surface. Roll the dough out to about 1/4-inch thickness.
- Using a sharp knife or pizza cutter, cut the dough into squares or rectangles, about 2-3 inches in size.

5. Fry the Beignets:

- In a large, deep skillet or Dutch oven, heat vegetable oil to 350°F (175°C). Carefully place a few pieces of dough into the hot oil, being careful not to overcrowd the pan.

- Fry the beignets for 1-2 minutes per side, or until golden brown and puffed up. Use a slotted spoon or spider strainer to remove the beignets from the oil and drain on a paper towel-lined plate or wire rack.

6. Serve:

- While still warm, generously dust the beignets with powdered sugar.
- Serve immediately and enjoy the beignets warm and fresh!

Tips:

- **Oil Temperature:** It's crucial to maintain the oil temperature around 350°F (175°C) for frying to ensure the beignets cook evenly and don't absorb too much oil.
- **Shape and Size:** Beignets can be traditionally square or rectangular, but you can also cut them into circles or other shapes. Ensure they are of similar size for even cooking.
- **Powdered Sugar:** The classic way to serve beignets is with a generous dusting of powdered sugar. You can also add a touch of cinnamon or nutmeg to the powdered sugar for extra flavor.
- **Enjoy Fresh:** Beignets are best enjoyed fresh and warm, soon after frying. They can be stored for a short time, but they are most delicious when served immediately.

Beignets are a wonderful treat for breakfast or dessert, loved for their light, fluffy texture and sweet powdered sugar coating. Enjoy making these French delicacies at home and share them with family and friends!

Flan Parisien

Ingredients:

For the Pastry Dough:

- 1 1/4 cups (160g) all-purpose flour
- 1/4 cup (50g) granulated sugar
- Pinch of salt
- 1/2 cup (115g) unsalted butter, cold and cut into cubes
- 1 large egg yolk
- 1-2 tablespoons ice water

For the Custard Filling:

- 2 cups (480ml) whole milk
- 1 cup (240ml) heavy cream
- 1 vanilla bean, split lengthwise (or 1 teaspoon vanilla extract)
- 4 large eggs
- 1 cup (200g) granulated sugar
- 1/2 cup (60g) cornstarch
- Zest of 1 lemon (optional)
- Pinch of salt

Instructions:

1. Prepare the Pastry Dough:

- In a food processor, combine the flour, sugar, and salt. Pulse to mix.
- Add the cold butter cubes and pulse until the mixture resembles coarse crumbs.
- Add the egg yolk and 1 tablespoon of ice water. Pulse again until the dough starts to come together. Add more ice water, 1 teaspoon at a time, if needed.
- Turn out the dough onto a lightly floured surface and gather into a ball. Flatten into a disc, wrap in plastic wrap, and refrigerate for at least 1 hour.

2. Pre-bake the Pastry Crust:

- Preheat your oven to 375°F (190°C).
- On a lightly floured surface, roll out the chilled pastry dough into a circle about 12 inches (30cm) in diameter. Carefully transfer the dough to a 9-inch (23cm) tart pan with a removable bottom. Press the dough into the pan and trim any excess.
- Prick the bottom of the pastry dough with a fork. Line the pastry with parchment paper or foil, and fill with pie weights or dried beans.

- Bake in the preheated oven for 15 minutes. Remove the parchment paper and weights, and bake for an additional 5-7 minutes, or until the pastry is lightly golden. Remove from the oven and let cool slightly.

3. Prepare the Custard Filling:

- In a saucepan, combine the whole milk, heavy cream, and split vanilla bean (scrape the seeds into the mixture) over medium heat. Heat until just simmering. Remove from heat and let it steep for about 10-15 minutes to infuse the flavors. If using vanilla extract, add it after steeping.
- In a large mixing bowl, whisk together the eggs, sugar, cornstarch, lemon zest (if using), and salt until smooth and pale yellow.
- Gradually whisk the warm milk mixture into the egg mixture, whisking constantly to prevent the eggs from scrambling.
- Pour the custard mixture through a fine-mesh sieve into a clean saucepan to remove any lumps or vanilla bean pieces.

4. Cook the Custard:

- Cook the custard mixture over medium heat, stirring constantly with a whisk, until thickened and just beginning to bubble, about 5-7 minutes.
- Remove from heat and continue stirring for another minute. The custard should be smooth and thick.

5. Assemble and Bake the Flan:

- Pour the hot custard filling into the pre-baked pastry crust, smoothing the top with a spatula.
- Return the tart to the oven and bake for 30-35 minutes, or until the custard is set and the top is golden brown.

6. Cool and Serve:

- Let the Flan Parisien cool completely in the tart pan on a wire rack. Once cooled, refrigerate for at least 2 hours, or until chilled and set.
- Serve slices of Flan Parisien cold or at room temperature. Dust with powdered sugar before serving, if desired.

Tips:

- **Vanilla Bean Substitution:** If you don't have a vanilla bean, you can use 1 teaspoon of vanilla extract instead. Add it after steeping the milk mixture.
- **Custard Consistency:** Stir the custard constantly while cooking to ensure a smooth texture and prevent lumps. It should be thick enough to coat the back of a spoon.
- **Make-Ahead:** Flan Parisien can be made a day in advance and stored in the refrigerator until ready to serve. This allows the flavors to meld and the custard to set fully.

Flan Parisien is a classic French dessert that combines the richness of a creamy custard with the buttery crispness of pastry crust. Enjoy making this elegant dessert at home and delight in its smooth, vanilla-infused flavor!

Pain d'Épices (French Spice Bread)

Ingredients:

- 1 cup (240ml) water
- 1 cup (340g) honey
- 1/2 cup (100g) granulated sugar
- Zest of 1 orange (optional)
- 2 cups (250g) all-purpose flour
- 1 cup (120g) whole wheat flour
- 1 tablespoon baking powder
- 1 teaspoon ground cinnamon
- 1 teaspoon ground ginger
- 1/2 teaspoon ground nutmeg
- 1/2 teaspoon ground cloves
- Pinch of salt

Instructions:

1. Prepare the Honey Mixture:

- In a small saucepan, combine the water, honey, granulated sugar, and orange zest (if using). Heat over medium heat, stirring occasionally, until the sugar dissolves and the mixture is smooth. Remove from heat and let cool slightly.

2. Mix the Dry Ingredients:

- In a large mixing bowl, whisk together the all-purpose flour, whole wheat flour, baking powder, ground cinnamon, ground ginger, ground nutmeg, ground cloves, and salt.

3. Combine Wet and Dry Ingredients:

- Gradually pour the cooled honey mixture into the dry ingredients, stirring with a wooden spoon or spatula until well combined and smooth. The batter will be thick.

4. Bake the Pain d'Épices:

- Preheat your oven to 325°F (160°C). Grease and flour a loaf pan (about 9x5 inches or 23x13 cm).
- Pour the batter into the prepared loaf pan, spreading it evenly with a spatula.
- Bake in the preheated oven for 50-60 minutes, or until a toothpick inserted into the center comes out clean or with a few moist crumbs.

5. Cool and Serve:

- Remove the Pain d'Épices from the oven and let it cool in the pan for 10-15 minutes. Then, transfer it to a wire rack to cool completely.
- Slice and serve the Pain d'Épices either warm or at room temperature. It's delicious on its own or served with butter, jam, or a spread of honey.

Tips:

- **Spice Variations:** Feel free to adjust the spices according to your preference. You can add a bit more cinnamon for a spicier flavor, or adjust the ginger and cloves to suit your taste.
- **Orange Zest:** The orange zest adds a lovely citrus aroma to the bread. If you prefer, you can omit it or substitute with lemon zest for a different citrus twist.
- **Storage:** Pain d'Épices keeps well at room temperature for a few days when wrapped tightly in plastic wrap or stored in an airtight container. It can also be frozen for longer storage.

Pain d'Épices is a delightful treat that embodies the warm flavors of cinnamon, ginger, and honey. Enjoy baking this traditional French spice bread and savor its comforting aroma and taste!

Saint-Honoré

Ingredients:

For the Pâte à Choux:

- 1/2 cup (120ml) water
- 1/2 cup (120ml) whole milk
- 1/2 cup (115g) unsalted butter, cut into cubes
- 1 tablespoon granulated sugar
- 1/4 teaspoon salt
- 1 cup (125g) all-purpose flour
- 4 large eggs

For the Whipped Cream:

- 1 cup (240ml) heavy cream, chilled
- 2 tablespoons powdered sugar
- 1 teaspoon vanilla extract

For Assembly:

- Puff pastry dough (store-bought or homemade)
- 1/2 cup (100g) granulated sugar
- 2 tablespoons water

Instructions:

1. Prepare the Pâte à Choux:

- Preheat your oven to 400°F (200°C). Line a baking sheet with parchment paper.
- In a medium saucepan, combine the water, milk, butter, sugar, and salt. Bring to a boil over medium-high heat.
- Reduce the heat to low and add the flour all at once. Stir vigorously with a wooden spoon until the mixture forms a smooth ball and pulls away from the sides of the pan. Cook for another 1-2 minutes to dry out the dough slightly.
- Transfer the dough to a mixing bowl or the bowl of a stand mixer fitted with a paddle attachment. Let it cool for a few minutes.
- Beat in the eggs one at a time, mixing well after each addition, until the dough is smooth and glossy.
- Transfer the choux pastry dough to a piping bag fitted with a large round tip (or simply cut the tip of the piping bag if using a disposable one).
- Pipe small rounds (about 1 inch in diameter) onto the prepared baking sheet, leaving space between each for spreading.

- Bake in the preheated oven for 15-20 minutes, or until the choux are puffed up and golden brown. Reduce the oven temperature to 350°F (175°C) after the first 10 minutes to ensure they bake evenly. Remove from the oven and let cool on a wire rack.

2. Prepare the Puff Pastry Base:

- Roll out your puff pastry dough to about 1/4 inch thick. Cut out a circle about 8-9 inches in diameter (you can use a cake ring or a plate as a guide). Prick the dough all over with a fork.
- Transfer the pastry circle to a baking sheet lined with parchment paper. Bake according to the package instructions or until golden brown and puffed. Let it cool completely on a wire rack.

3. Make the Caramel for Assembly:

- In a small saucepan, combine the granulated sugar and water over medium heat. Swirl the pan gently (do not stir) until the sugar dissolves.
- Increase the heat to medium-high and cook until the mixture turns a deep amber color, swirling the pan occasionally to ensure even caramelization. Remove from heat immediately to prevent burning.
- Working quickly and carefully (as caramel is very hot), dip the bottoms of the baked choux pastries into the caramel and place them, caramel side down, around the edge of the puff pastry base. This creates a crown-like border of choux.

4. Fill the Choux with Whipped Cream:

- In a chilled bowl, whip the heavy cream with powdered sugar and vanilla extract until stiff peaks form.
- Fill each choux pastry with the whipped cream using a piping bag fitted with a small round tip or simply cut a small hole in the side of each pastry and spoon in the cream.

5. Serve and Enjoy:

- Serve the Saint-Honoré immediately or refrigerate until ready to serve. It's best enjoyed fresh to maintain the crispness of the puff pastry and the lightness of the whipped cream.

Tips:

- **Pâte à Choux Consistency:** The choux pastry dough should be smooth and glossy, with a pipeable consistency. If it's too stiff, add a little more beaten egg.
- **Caramel Handling:** Be cautious when working with caramel, as it can cause serious burns. Work quickly and mindfully when dipping the choux pastries.
- **Variations:** Saint-Honoré can be customized with different fillings such as pastry cream or flavored whipped creams. You can also add a drizzle of chocolate ganache over the whipped cream for added richness.

Saint-Honoré is a stunning and delicious French dessert that requires a bit of technique but is well worth the effort for special occasions. Enjoy making this classic pastry and delight in its combination of textures and flavors!

Navettes de Marseille

Ingredients:

- 2 cups (250g) all-purpose flour
- 1/2 cup (100g) granulated sugar
- 1/2 teaspoon baking powder
- Pinch of salt
- Zest of 1 organic orange
- 1/4 cup (60ml) vegetable oil
- 1/4 cup (60ml) milk
- 2 tablespoons orange blossom water
- 1 egg yolk, beaten (for brushing)
- Granulated sugar, for sprinkling

Instructions:

1. Prepare the Dough:

- Preheat your oven to 350°F (175°C). Line a baking sheet with parchment paper.
- In a large mixing bowl, whisk together the flour, sugar, baking powder, salt, and orange zest.
- In a separate bowl, whisk together the vegetable oil, milk, and orange blossom water.
- Gradually add the wet ingredients to the dry ingredients, stirring with a wooden spoon or spatula until the dough comes together. If the dough is too dry, add a little more milk, a teaspoon at a time, until it forms a smooth ball.

2. Shape the Navettes:

- Divide the dough into 4 equal portions. On a lightly floured surface, roll each portion into a rope about 1/2 inch (1.5 cm) thick.
- Cut each rope into pieces about 4 inches (10 cm) long. Gently press each piece with your fingers to flatten slightly and shape into a boat-like form, tapering the ends.
- Place the shaped navettes onto the prepared baking sheet, leaving space between each.

3. Bake the Navettes:

- Brush the tops of the navettes with beaten egg yolk and sprinkle generously with granulated sugar.
- Bake in the preheated oven for 15-18 minutes, or until the navettes are golden brown and firm to the touch.

4. Cool and Serve:

- Remove the navettes from the oven and let them cool on a wire rack.
- Once cooled, store the navettes in an airtight container at room temperature. They can be enjoyed plain or with tea, coffee, or dessert wine.

Tips:

- **Orange Blossom Water:** Orange blossom water is a key ingredient that gives navettes their distinctive flavor. It can usually be found in specialty grocery stores or online. Adjust the amount according to your taste preference.
- **Storage:** Navettes can be stored in an airtight container at room temperature for up to a week. They may become slightly softer over time but will still be delicious.
- **Variations:** Some recipes may include additional flavors such as vanilla or lemon zest. Feel free to experiment with different citrus flavors or spices to customize the navettes to your liking.

Navettes de Marseille are a delightful treat with a rich history, perfect for enjoying as a snack or serving alongside a cup of tea. Their unique boat-like shape and fragrant orange blossom flavor make them a special addition to any dessert table. Enjoy baking and savoring these traditional French biscuits!

Tuiles

Ingredients:

- 1/2 cup (115g) unsalted butter, melted
- 1/2 cup (100g) granulated sugar
- 1/4 teaspoon vanilla extract
- Pinch of salt
- 2 large egg whites
- 1/2 cup (60g) all-purpose flour
- 1/2 cup (50g) sliced almonds (optional, for almond tuiles)
- Zest of 1 lemon or orange (optional, for citrus-flavored tuiles)
- Cocoa powder (optional, for chocolate tuiles)

Instructions:

1. Prepare the Batter:

- In a mixing bowl, combine the melted butter, sugar, vanilla extract, and salt. Stir until the sugar is dissolved.
- Add the egg whites and whisk until smooth.
- Gradually add the flour and mix until well combined. The batter should have a smooth consistency. If making flavored tuiles, add the lemon or orange zest or cocoa powder at this stage and mix well.
- If adding sliced almonds, fold them gently into the batter.

2. Chill the Batter:

- Cover the bowl with plastic wrap and refrigerate the batter for at least 1 hour, or until it firms up. This chilling step helps the batter to rest and develop flavor.

3. Preheat the Oven:

- Preheat your oven to 350°F (175°C). Line a baking sheet with parchment paper.

4. Shape the Tuiles:

- Spoon small amounts of batter (about 1 tablespoon) onto the prepared baking sheet, leaving space between each for spreading. Use the back of a spoon or an offset spatula to spread the batter into thin, even circles or ovals. Aim for a thickness of about 1/8 inch (3mm).

5. Bake the Tuiles:

- Bake in the preheated oven for 8-10 minutes, or until the edges of the tuiles are golden brown. Keep a close eye on them as they can quickly over-brown.

6. Shape the Tuiles:

- Working quickly while the tuiles are still warm and flexible, use a spatula to lift each tuile and shape it over a rolling pin, a cup, or a curved mold to create the characteristic curved shape. If you prefer flat tuiles, you can leave them to cool on the baking sheet.

7. Cool and Serve:

- Transfer the shaped tuiles to a wire rack to cool completely. They will crisp up as they cool.
- Repeat the baking process with the remaining batter, making sure to cool the baking sheet between batches.

8. Store:

- Once completely cooled, store the tuiles in an airtight container at room temperature. They should stay crispy for several days.

Tips:

- **Shaping Tuiles:** Work quickly to shape the tuiles while they are warm and flexible. If they become too firm to shape, you can briefly return them to the oven for a few seconds to soften.

- **Flavor Variations:** Tuiles can be flavored with various ingredients such as citrus zest (lemon or orange), cocoa powder for chocolate tuiles, or even ground spices like cinnamon or cardamom for a spiced version.
- **Presentation:** Tuiles are often served on their own as a crisp, delicate cookie, or they can be used to garnish desserts such as ice cream, mousses, or fruit salads. They add a delightful crunch and elegance to any dessert presentation.

Enjoy making these delicate and crispy tuiles at home! They are a versatile treat that pairs beautifully with a variety of flavors and can be enjoyed on their own or as a sophisticated garnish.

Petits Fours

Components of Petits Fours:

1. **Cake Base:**
    - Choose a light and moist cake base such as genoise (sponge cake), madeleine batter, or even a dense pound cake. These cakes are baked in thin layers or small molds to create a base for the petits fours.
2. **Fillings:**
    - Petits fours can be filled with various creams, jams, or ganaches. For example, you might use pastry cream, fruit preserves, chocolate ganache, or flavored buttercream.
3. **Coatings:**
    - After assembling and filling the petits fours, they are often coated with a thin layer of icing, glaze, fondant, or chocolate ganache. This adds flavor and a smooth finish to the petits fours.
4. **Decoration:**
    - Petits fours are elegantly decorated with piped designs, candied fruit, nuts, chocolate drizzles, or edible flowers. This step adds visual appeal and enhances the overall presentation.

Steps to Make Petits Fours:

1. Bake the Cake Base:

- Choose your desired cake recipe and bake it in thin layers or small molds. Let the cakes cool completely before proceeding.

2. Prepare the Fillings:

- Make your fillings such as pastry cream, ganache, or fruit preserves. These will be used to sandwich the cake layers or fill molded petits fours.

3. Assemble the Petits Fours:

- Trim the cake layers into uniform sizes and spread a thin layer of filling between each layer. Stack them neatly and trim the edges for a clean finish.

4. Coat with Glaze or Fondant:

- Prepare a glaze or fondant icing suitable for petits fours. Dip each assembled petit four into the glaze or pour it over them to coat evenly. Let them set on a wire rack.

5. Decorate:

- Once the glaze or fondant has set slightly, decorate the petits fours with piped designs, chocolate drizzles, candied fruits, nuts, or other decorative elements. Let them set completely before serving.

Tips for Making Petits Fours:

- **Precision:** Work carefully and precisely, as petits fours require attention to detail, especially when assembling and decorating.
- **Chilling:** Chill the assembled petits fours before cutting them into small, bite-sized pieces to ensure clean cuts.
- **Variety:** Experiment with different cake bases, fillings, and decorations to create a variety of petits fours with unique flavors and textures.
- **Storage:** Store petits fours in an airtight container in a cool place. They can be made ahead of time and refrigerated or frozen, depending on the type of filling and icing used.

Petits fours are a delightful treat that showcase the artistry and craftsmanship of French pastry making. Enjoy the process of creating these miniature delights and savor the elegant flavors they bring to any dessert table or special occasion!

Opéra Cake

Components of Opéra Cake:

1. **Almond Joconde (Almond Sponge Cake):**
   - This forms the base of the Opéra Cake and is made with almond flour, eggs, sugar, and a small amount of flour for structure.
2. **Coffee Buttercream:**
   - A smooth and creamy buttercream flavored with coffee or espresso. It adds richness and complements the almond sponge cake layers.
3. **Chocolate Ganache:**
   - A mixture of chocolate and cream, used to add a luxurious layer of chocolate flavor between the almond sponge cake layers.
4. **Chocolate Glaze:**
   - A shiny chocolate glaze that covers the entire cake, providing a smooth finish and enhancing the overall presentation.

Ingredients:

For the Almond Joconde:

- 3 large eggs, at room temperature
- 3 large egg whites, at room temperature
- 1/2 cup (60g) almond flour
- 1/2 cup (60g) powdered sugar
- 1/4 cup (30g) all-purpose flour
- 1 tablespoon unsalted butter, melted and cooled
- 2 tablespoons granulated sugar

For the Coffee Buttercream:

- 1/2 cup (120ml) strong brewed coffee or espresso
- 1 cup (200g) granulated sugar
- 4 large egg yolks
- 1 cup (225g) unsalted butter, softened
- 1 teaspoon vanilla extract

For the Chocolate Ganache:

- 4 ounces (115g) dark chocolate, finely chopped
- 1/2 cup (120ml) heavy cream

For the Chocolate Glaze:

- 4 ounces (115g) dark chocolate, finely chopped

- 1/2 cup (120ml) heavy cream
- 1 tablespoon unsalted butter, softened

Instructions:

1. Make the Almond Joconde:

- Preheat your oven to 350°F (175°C). Grease a 9x13-inch (23x33cm) baking pan and line it with parchment paper.
- In a large bowl, beat the eggs and egg whites with granulated sugar until thick and pale, about 5 minutes.
- Sift together the almond flour, powdered sugar, and all-purpose flour. Gently fold the dry ingredients into the egg mixture.
- Fold in the melted butter until fully incorporated.
- Spread the batter evenly into the prepared baking pan. Bake for 12-15 minutes, or until the cake springs back when lightly touched. Let it cool completely in the pan.

2. Prepare the Coffee Buttercream:

- In a small saucepan, heat the coffee or espresso until simmering. Remove from heat.
- In a heatproof bowl, whisk together the sugar and egg yolks. Gradually whisk in the hot coffee.
- Place the bowl over a pot of simmering water (double boiler) and cook, whisking constantly, until the mixture thickens and reaches 160°F (71°C) on a thermometer.
- Remove from heat and let cool to room temperature.
- In a separate bowl, beat the softened butter until creamy. Gradually add the cooled coffee mixture, beating until smooth and fluffy. Stir in vanilla extract. Set aside.

3. Make the Chocolate Ganache:

- Place the chopped chocolate in a heatproof bowl.
- In a small saucepan, heat the cream until it just begins to boil. Pour the hot cream over the chopped chocolate and let it sit for 1-2 minutes.
- Gently stir until the chocolate is melted and smooth. Let it cool slightly.

4. Assemble the Opéra Cake:

- Cut the cooled almond joconde into three equal-sized rectangles (about 9x4 inches each).
- Place one rectangle of almond joconde on a serving platter or cake board. Spread half of the coffee buttercream evenly over the cake.
- Place another rectangle of almond joconde on top and press gently to adhere. Spread the chocolate ganache evenly over this layer.
- Top with the final rectangle of almond joconde. Press gently to adhere.

5. Prepare the Chocolate Glaze:

- Place the chopped chocolate in a heatproof bowl.
- In a small saucepan, heat the cream until it just begins to boil. Pour the hot cream over the chopped chocolate and let it sit for 1-2 minutes.
- Gently stir until the chocolate is melted and smooth. Stir in the softened butter until smooth and glossy.

6. Finish the Opéra Cake:

- Pour the warm chocolate glaze over the top of the assembled cake, spreading it evenly with an offset spatula to cover the entire surface.
- Refrigerate the Opéra Cake for at least 2 hours, or until the glaze is set and the cake is firm.

7. Serve and Enjoy:

- Use a sharp knife dipped in hot water and wiped clean to slice the Opéra Cake into small rectangles or squares. Serve chilled.

Tips:

- **Assembly:** Take your time with each layer to ensure even spreading of the buttercream and ganache for a balanced cake.
- **Chilling:** Allowing the cake to chill after assembly helps the flavors meld together and makes it easier to slice cleanly.
- **Decoration:** If desired, you can decorate the top of the Opéra Cake with chocolate shavings, gold leaf, or edible flowers for an elegant finish.

Opéra Cake requires a bit of effort but is well worth it for its sophisticated layers of flavor and texture. It's a show-stopping dessert that is sure to impress at any special occasion. Enjoy making and indulging in this French pastry masterpiece!

Cherry Clafoutis

Ingredients:

- 1 cup (240ml) whole milk
- 1/2 cup (100g) granulated sugar
- 3 large eggs
- 1 tablespoon vanilla extract
- 1/8 teaspoon salt
- 1/2 cup (65g) all-purpose flour
- 2 cups (300g) fresh cherries, pitted
- Powdered sugar, for dusting

Instructions:

1. Preheat the Oven:

- Preheat your oven to 350°F (175°C). Grease a 9-inch (23cm) pie dish or baking dish with butter.

2. Prepare the Cherries:

- Wash the cherries, remove the stems, and pit them using a cherry pitter or a small knife. You can leave the cherries whole or halve them if you prefer.

3. Make the Batter:

- In a blender or using a whisk, combine the milk, granulated sugar, eggs, vanilla extract, salt, and flour. Blend or whisk until the mixture is smooth and well combined. Let the batter rest for about 15 minutes to allow the flour to hydrate.

4. Assemble the Clafoutis:

- Arrange the pitted cherries in a single layer in the prepared pie dish.
- Pour the batter over the cherries, covering them evenly.

5. Bake the Clafoutis:

- Place the pie dish in the preheated oven and bake for 35-40 minutes, or until the clafoutis is set and golden brown on top. It should be puffed up and slightly jiggly in the center.

6. Cool and Serve:

- Remove the clafoutis from the oven and let it cool for about 10 minutes before serving.

- Dust the clafoutis with powdered sugar just before serving. It can be served warm, at room temperature, or chilled.

Tips:

- **Cherry Variations:** While traditionally made with whole cherries, you can also use other fruits such as berries or sliced stone fruits like peaches or plums.
- **Flavor Variations:** Add a splash of almond extract or a tablespoon of kirsch (cherry liqueur) to the batter for extra flavor.
- **Texture:** The texture of clafoutis should be somewhere between a custard and a pancake. It's normal for it to deflate slightly as it cools.
- **Serving Suggestions:** Enjoy Cherry Clafoutis on its own or with a dollop of whipped cream, a scoop of vanilla ice cream, or a drizzle of crème fraîche for a delightful dessert.

Cherry Clafoutis is a wonderful way to celebrate the sweetness of fresh cherries in a simple and elegant dessert. It's perfect for any occasion, from casual family dinners to special gatherings with friends.

Croquembouche

Ingredients:

For the Choux Pastry:

- 1/2 cup (120ml) water
- 1/2 cup (120ml) whole milk
- 1/2 cup (115g) unsalted butter, cut into cubes
- 1 tablespoon granulated sugar
- 1/4 teaspoon salt
- 1 cup (125g) all-purpose flour
- 4 large eggs, at room temperature

For the Pastry Cream:

- 2 cups (480ml) whole milk
- 1/2 cup (100g) granulated sugar
- 4 large egg yolks
- 1/4 cup (30g) cornstarch
- 2 tablespoons unsalted butter
- 1 teaspoon vanilla extract

For the Caramel:

- 2 cups (400g) granulated sugar
- 1/2 cup (120ml) water

For Assembly and Decoration:

- Cooled choux pastry puffs
- Prepared pastry cream
- Prepared caramel
- Optional: Edible flowers, spun sugar, or decorative elements for garnish

Instructions:

1. Make the Choux Pastry:

- Preheat your oven to 400°F (200°C). Line a baking sheet with parchment paper.
- In a medium saucepan, combine water, milk, butter, sugar, and salt. Bring to a boil over medium-high heat.
- Reduce the heat to low and add the flour all at once. Stir vigorously with a wooden spoon until the mixture forms a smooth ball and pulls away from the sides of the pan. Cook for another 1-2 minutes to dry out the dough slightly.

- Transfer the dough to a mixing bowl or the bowl of a stand mixer fitted with a paddle attachment. Let it cool for a few minutes.
- Beat in the eggs one at a time, mixing well after each addition, until the dough is smooth and glossy.
- Transfer the choux pastry dough to a piping bag fitted with a large round tip (or simply cut the tip of the piping bag if using a disposable one).
- Pipe small rounds (about 1 inch in diameter) onto the prepared baking sheet, leaving space between each for spreading.
- Bake in the preheated oven for 15-20 minutes, or until the choux are puffed up and golden brown. Reduce the oven temperature to 350°F (175°C) after the first 10 minutes to ensure they bake evenly. Remove from the oven and let cool on a wire rack.

2. Prepare the Pastry Cream:

- In a medium saucepan, heat the milk until steaming (do not boil).
- In a separate bowl, whisk together the sugar, egg yolks, and cornstarch until smooth and pale.
- Gradually whisk the hot milk into the egg mixture to temper it.
- Return the mixture to the saucepan and cook over medium heat, whisking constantly, until thickened and bubbling. Remove from heat.
- Stir in the butter and vanilla extract until smooth. Transfer to a bowl and cover the surface with plastic wrap to prevent a skin from forming. Chill in the refrigerator until completely cool.

3. Fill the Choux Pastry:

- Using a piping bag fitted with a small round tip, fill each choux pastry puff with the chilled pastry cream. Insert the tip into the base of each puff and gently squeeze until filled.

4. Assemble the Croquembouche:

- Prepare the caramel by heating sugar and water in a saucepan over medium-high heat. Swirl the pan occasionally until the sugar dissolves. Cook until the mixture turns a deep amber color, then remove from heat immediately.
- Carefully dip the top of each filled choux pastry puff into the caramel and stick them together in a cone shape on a serving platter or cake stand. Work quickly before the caramel hardens.
- Continue layering the puffs in a pyramid shape until you achieve the desired height and shape of the Croquembouche.

5. Decorate:

- Drizzle any remaining caramel over the top of the Croquembouche for a decorative effect. You can also add spun sugar, edible flowers, or other decorations as desired.

6. Serve:

- Croquembouche is best served fresh, while the caramel is still crispy and the pastry cream inside the puffs is chilled and creamy. Use a sharp knife to slice and serve individual portions.

Tips:

- **Handling Caramel:** Be extremely careful when working with hot caramel as it can cause severe burns. Work quickly and use caution throughout the caramel-making process.
- **Assembly:** Assemble the Croquembouche just before serving to maintain its structure and freshness.
- **Variations:** You can customize your Croquembouche with different flavors of pastry cream, such as chocolate or coffee, or by adding crushed nuts or flavored whipped cream.

Croquembouche is a show-stopping dessert that requires some effort but is guaranteed to impress guests with its elegant appearance and delightful combination of crispy caramel, creamy pastry cream, and light choux pastry. Enjoy creating this French masterpiece for special celebrations!

Brioche aux Pralines

Ingredients:

For the Brioche Dough:

- 2 cups (250g) all-purpose flour
- 3 tablespoons granulated sugar
- 1 teaspoon salt
- 1 tablespoon active dry yeast
- 1/2 cup (120ml) warm milk
- 3 large eggs, at room temperature
- 1/2 cup (115g) unsalted butter, softened
- 1 teaspoon vanilla extract

For the Pralines:

- 1 cup (200g) granulated sugar
- 1/2 cup (120ml) water
- 1 cup (150g) whole almonds (or hazelnuts), toasted and roughly chopped

For Assembly:

- Prepared brioche dough
- Prepared pralines
- Egg wash (1 egg beaten with 1 tablespoon of water)
- Pearl sugar or coarse sugar (optional, for sprinkling)

Instructions:

1. Prepare the Brioche Dough:

- In a small bowl, dissolve the yeast and 1 tablespoon of sugar in warm milk. Let it sit for about 5-10 minutes until foamy.
- In the bowl of a stand mixer fitted with the dough hook attachment, combine the flour, remaining sugar, and salt.
- Add the yeast mixture, eggs, and vanilla extract to the flour mixture. Mix on low speed until the dough starts to come together.
- Increase the speed to medium and knead the dough for about 5 minutes, or until it becomes smooth and elastic.
- Gradually add the softened butter, a few tablespoons at a time, until it is fully incorporated and the dough is smooth and shiny.
- Cover the bowl with plastic wrap and let the dough rise in a warm place for about 1-2 hours, or until it doubles in size.

2. Prepare the Pralines:

- Line a baking sheet with parchment paper and set aside.
- In a saucepan, combine the granulated sugar and water over medium heat. Stir until the sugar dissolves.
- Increase the heat to medium-high and cook the syrup, without stirring, until it reaches a deep amber color (about 320°F or 160°C on a candy thermometer).
- Remove the saucepan from the heat and quickly stir in the toasted chopped almonds.
- Immediately pour the praline mixture onto the prepared baking sheet, spreading it out into a thin layer. Let it cool completely.
- Once cooled, break the praline into small pieces or roughly chop it into chunks.

3. Assemble the Brioche aux Pralines:

- Preheat your oven to 350°F (175°C). Grease and line a loaf pan with parchment paper.
- Punch down the risen brioche dough and transfer it to a lightly floured surface. Gently knead in about 3/4 cup of the chopped pralines, distributing them evenly throughout the dough.
- Shape the dough into a loaf shape and place it into the prepared loaf pan. Cover loosely with plastic wrap and let it rise again for about 30-45 minutes, or until it puffs up.
- Brush the top of the brioche loaf with the egg wash and sprinkle with pearl sugar or coarse sugar if desired.
- Bake in the preheated oven for 30-35 minutes, or until the top is golden brown and the brioche sounds hollow when tapped on the bottom.
- Remove from the oven and let the brioche cool in the pan for 10 minutes before transferring it to a wire rack to cool completely.

4. Serve and Enjoy:

- Slice the Brioche aux Pralines and serve it warm or at room temperature. Enjoy the buttery richness of the brioche with the sweet crunch of caramelized pralines.

Tips:

- **Toasting Nuts:** Toasting the almonds (or hazelnuts) adds depth of flavor to the pralines. Spread them in a single layer on a baking sheet and toast in a preheated oven at 350°F (175°C) for about 8-10 minutes, or until fragrant and lightly browned.
- **Storage:** Store any leftover Brioche aux Pralines in an airtight container at room temperature for up to 2-3 days. It can also be frozen for longer storage.

Brioche aux Pralines is a decadent treat that combines the best of both worlds – the soft, buttery texture of brioche with the sweet and crunchy pralines. Enjoy this delightful pastry with a cup of coffee or tea for a special breakfast or afternoon snack!

Tarte Tropézienne

Ingredients:

For the Brioche Dough:

- 2 cups (250g) all-purpose flour
- 3 tablespoons granulated sugar
- 1 teaspoon salt
- 1 tablespoon active dry yeast
- 1/2 cup (120ml) warm milk
- 3 large eggs, at room temperature
- 1/2 cup (115g) unsalted butter, softened
- 1 teaspoon vanilla extract
- Zest of 1 lemon (optional)

For the Pastry Cream:

- 1 cup (240ml) whole milk
- 4 large egg yolks
- 1/4 cup (50g) granulated sugar
- 2 tablespoons cornstarch
- 1 teaspoon vanilla extract
- 1 cup (240ml) heavy cream, chilled

For the Sugar Syrup:

- 1/4 cup (50g) granulated sugar
- 1/4 cup (60ml) water
- 1 tablespoon rum (optional)

For Assembly:

- Prepared brioche dough
- Prepared pastry cream
- Powdered sugar, for dusting

Instructions:

1. Make the Brioche Dough:

- In a small bowl, dissolve the yeast and 1 tablespoon of sugar in warm milk. Let it sit for about 5-10 minutes until foamy.
- In the bowl of a stand mixer fitted with the dough hook attachment, combine the flour, remaining sugar, salt, and lemon zest (if using).

- Add the yeast mixture, eggs, and vanilla extract to the flour mixture. Mix on low speed until the dough starts to come together.
- Increase the speed to medium and knead the dough for about 5 minutes, or until it becomes smooth and elastic.
- Gradually add the softened butter, a few tablespoons at a time, until it is fully incorporated and the dough is smooth and shiny.
- Cover the bowl with plastic wrap and let the dough rise in a warm place for about 1-2 hours, or until it doubles in size.

2. Bake the Brioche:

- Punch down the risen dough and transfer it to a lightly floured surface. Shape it into a round or oval shape (about 8-9 inches in diameter) and place it on a baking sheet lined with parchment paper.
- Cover loosely with plastic wrap and let it rise again for about 30-45 minutes, or until it puffs up.
- Preheat your oven to 375°F (190°C).
- Bake the brioche in the preheated oven for 20-25 minutes, or until it is golden brown and sounds hollow when tapped on the bottom.
- Remove from the oven and let it cool completely on a wire rack.

3. Prepare the Pastry Cream:

- In a medium saucepan, heat the milk until steaming (do not boil).
- In a separate bowl, whisk together the egg yolks, sugar, and cornstarch until smooth and pale.
- Gradually whisk the hot milk into the egg mixture to temper it.
- Return the mixture to the saucepan and cook over medium heat, whisking constantly, until thickened and bubbling. Remove from heat.
- Stir in the vanilla extract. Transfer the pastry cream to a bowl and cover the surface with plastic wrap to prevent a skin from forming. Chill in the refrigerator until completely cool.
- In a separate bowl, whip the heavy cream until stiff peaks form. Gently fold the whipped cream into the chilled pastry cream until smooth and combined. This lightens the pastry cream and makes it creamy.

4. Make the Sugar Syrup:

- In a small saucepan, combine the sugar and water over medium heat. Stir until the sugar dissolves.
- Remove from heat and stir in the rum (if using). Let the syrup cool completely.

5. Assemble the Tarte Tropézienne:

- Using a serrated knife, carefully slice the cooled brioche horizontally into two even layers.
- Brush the cut sides of both brioche layers generously with the cooled sugar syrup.

- Spread the prepared pastry cream evenly over the bottom layer of the brioche.
- Gently place the top layer of brioche over the pastry cream, pressing down lightly.

6. Serve and Enjoy:

- Dust the top of the Tarte Tropézienne with powdered sugar.
- Chill the assembled Tarte Tropézienne in the refrigerator for at least 1 hour before serving to allow the flavors to meld together.
- Slice into wedges and serve chilled. Enjoy this delightful French dessert!

Tips:

- **Variations:** Some versions of Tarte Tropézienne use a simple whipped cream filling instead of pastry cream. You can adjust the filling according to your preference.
- **Decoration:** Garnish with fresh berries or candied fruit on top for added color and flavor.
- **Storage:** Store any leftover Tarte Tropézienne in the refrigerator, covered, for up to 2-3 days. It's best enjoyed fresh, but it can be kept for a short period.

Tarte Tropézienne is a wonderful treat that combines the soft, buttery richness of brioche with the creamy decadence of pastry cream or whipped cream. It's perfect for special occasions or any time you want to indulge in a taste of French elegance!

Pâte Feuilletée (Puff Pastry)

Ingredients:

- 2 1/2 cups (320g) all-purpose flour, plus extra for dusting
- 1 teaspoon salt
- 1 cup (240ml) cold water
- 1 cup (230g) unsalted butter, chilled but pliable
- Extra flour, for dusting

Instructions:

1. Prepare the Dough:

- In a large bowl, mix the flour and salt together.
- Gradually add the cold water, mixing until the dough comes together. It should be a rough, shaggy mass. If needed, add a little more water, but be cautious not to make it too wet.
- Turn the dough out onto a lightly floured surface and knead briefly until smooth. Shape it into a square, wrap it in plastic wrap, and refrigerate for 30 minutes.

2. Prepare the Butter Block:

- Place the chilled butter on a sheet of plastic wrap. Fold the plastic wrap over the butter and use a rolling pin to pound and roll the butter into a square about 1/2 inch thick. This helps soften the butter and makes it pliable without melting it.
- Once the butter is pliable, remove it from the plastic wrap and place it between two sheets of parchment paper. Roll it out into a square about 8 inches (20 cm) across. If the butter becomes too soft, refrigerate it until firm but still pliable.

3. Laminate the Dough:

- On a lightly floured surface, roll out the chilled dough into a square about 10 inches (25 cm) across. Place the butter square diagonally on the dough square, so it forms a diamond shape.
- Fold the corners of the dough over the butter to encase it completely, pinching the seams together to seal.
- Roll out the dough into a rectangle about 8 x 24 inches (20 x 60 cm). The butter should be evenly distributed and not breaking through the dough.
- Fold the dough into thirds like a business letter: bring the bottom third up, then fold the top third down over it. This completes the first "turn".
- Rotate the dough 90 degrees so the open side is facing you. Roll out the dough again into a rectangle and fold it into thirds again. This completes the second "turn".

- Repeat this rolling and folding process (rolling out, folding into thirds) two more times for a total of four "turns". This creates layers in the dough and forms the characteristic flakiness of puff pastry.

4. Chill and Rest:

- Wrap the puff pastry dough tightly in plastic wrap and refrigerate for at least 1 hour or overnight. This allows the dough to relax and chill completely before using.

5. Use or Freeze:

- Use the puff pastry as directed in your recipe, rolling it out to the desired thickness and shape. Alternatively, if not using immediately, wrap tightly in plastic wrap and store in the refrigerator for up to 2 days, or freeze for up to 3 months.

Tips for Success:

- **Temperature Control:** Keep the dough and butter cold throughout the process to prevent the butter from melting into the dough.
- **Even Rolling:** Roll the dough out evenly to maintain consistent layers. Avoid overworking the dough to prevent gluten development.
- **Resting Time:** Allow the dough to rest and chill between each turn to relax the gluten and ensure the layers form properly.
- **Freezing:** If freezing, thaw puff pastry in the refrigerator overnight before using.

Making puff pastry from scratch requires patience and precision, but the result is a wonderfully flaky and buttery pastry that can be used for both sweet and savory dishes. Enjoy experimenting with different fillings and shapes once you've mastered this basic technique!

www.ingramcontent.com/pod-product-compliance
Lightning Source LLC
LaVergne TN
LVHW061938070526
838199LV00060B/3864